C0-AWS-231

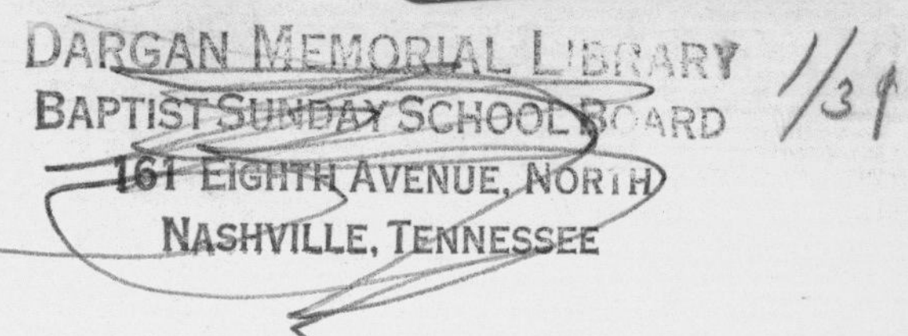

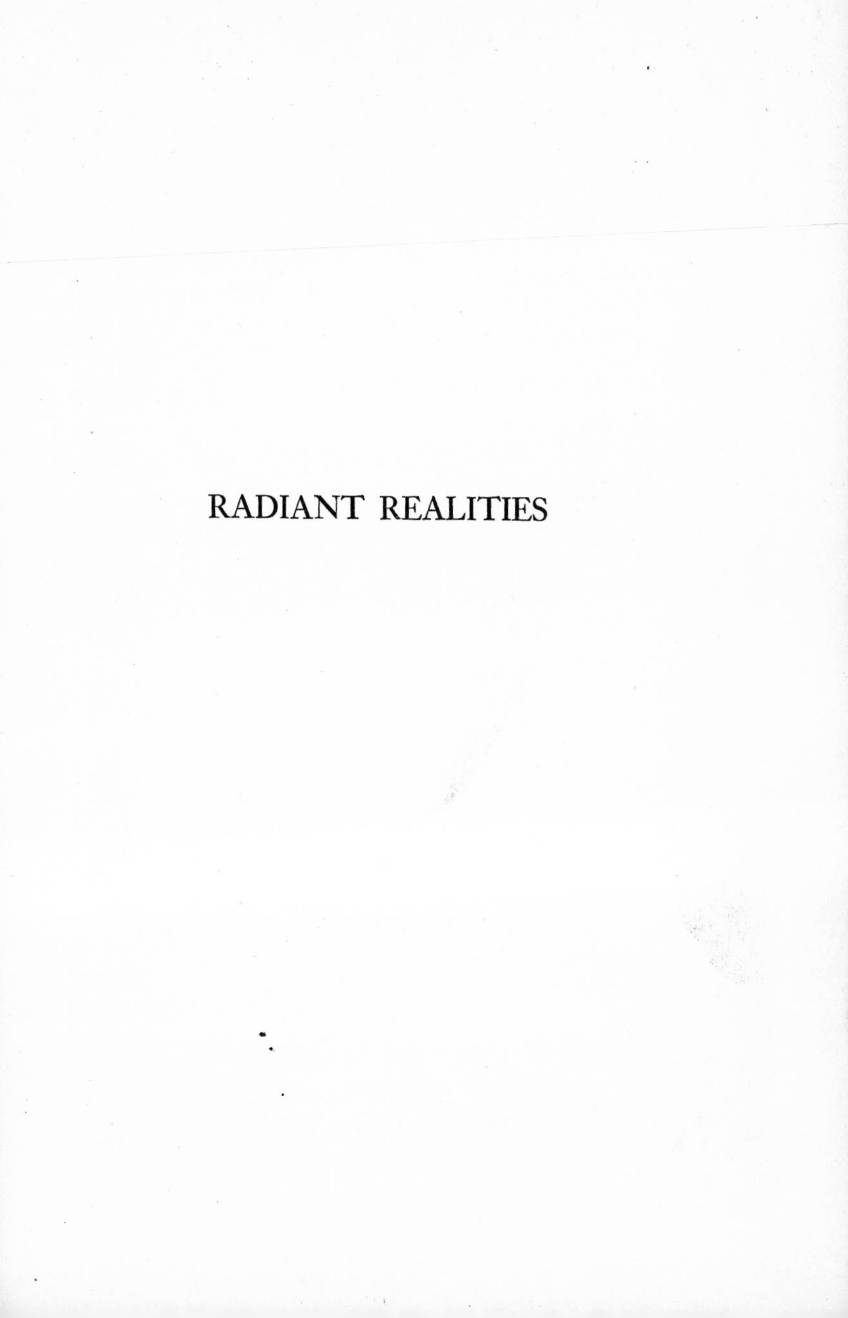

RADIANT REALITIES

RADIANT REALITIES

David Marshall Gardner, D.D.
Pastor, First Baptist Church
St. Petersburg, Florida
Author of *A Rainbow For Every Cloud*

RADIANT REALITIES

By

DAVID MARSHALL GARDNER, D.D.

BROADMAN PRESS
NASHVILLE, TENNESSEE

This volume is affectionately dedicated to our three children, Sadie Rae, David M., Jr., and Edith Marie, whose radiant personalities and noble Christian characters have been a joy and an inspiration through the years.

CONTENTS

PREFACE

These sermons have been prepared under the pressure of multiform duties incident to being pastor of a church in the heart of a tourist city. We minister to mighty multitudes of visitors from all sections of the world. St. Petersburg claims to be and is known throughout the nation as "the church-going city." The fact that we have had, by actual count, as many as forty-one states and four foreign countries represented in a Saturday evening service is sufficient confirmation of the claim.

People come here from everywhere and bring with them all types and shades of religious principles, prejudices, and preconceived notions. Yet to offset that fact, it is our privilege to minister to great throngs of the most refined, cultured, and consecrated Christians of the nation. Dr. George W. Truett was speaking from our pulpit when he said: "A testimony for Christ from this pulpit will have a more far-reaching influence for good than a similar testimony given from any other pulpit in America."

If the messages of this volume have real merit, they derive their value from the fact that they deal with vital themes of the Christian religion in a plain and practical way. Hence, they are sent forth in printed form, because of a conviction that the world needs the truths and testimonies contained in them.

Last, but not least, I wish thus to acknowledge my gratitude to the reading public for the generous reception given to my *A Rainbow For Every Cloud*.

DAVID M. GARDNER.

Chapter 1

RADIANT REALITIES

> For our light affliction, which is but for a moment, worketh for us a far more exceeding and eternal weight of glory; while we look not at the things which are seen, but at the things which are not seen: for the things which are seen are temporal; but the things which are not seen are eternal.—2 CORINTHIANS 4: 17, 18.

JOHN RUSKIN says: "The more I think of it, I find this conclusion more impressed upon me, that the greatest thing a human soul ever does in this world is to see something, and tell what it saw in a plain way. Hundreds of people can talk for one who can think; but thousands can think for one who can see. To see clearly is poetry, prophecy, and religion—all in one."

Paul is doing exactly what Ruskin calls "the greatest thing a human soul can do." He has pondered and thought straight through some of the deep things of the Spirit and is telling us of the rich and radiant realities he has seen over on the other side. He is not speaking as a blind optimist, but as an intelligent believer. His optimism is based upon an intelligent investigation plus personal experience and close observation. He had evidently investigated the case of David and employs David's very words in defense of his own strong declaration of faith. David declared:

"I believed, therefore have I spoken" (Psalm 116: 10). Paul speaks for himself and all others who have "the same spirit of faith," when he asserts: "We also believe, and therefore speak" (2 Cor. 4: 13). He speaks not as a materialistic stoic, nor as a "pink tea" philosopher, but as a Christian. He knew suffering and the meaning of it. "Are they ministers of Christ? (I speak as a fool) I am more; in labours more abundant, in stripes above measure, in prisons more frequent, in deaths oft. Of the Jews five times received I forty stripes save one. Thrice was I beaten with rods, once was I stoned, thrice I suffered shipwreck, a night and a day I have been in the deep; in journeyings often, in perils of waters, in perils of robbers, in perils by mine own countrymen, in perils by the heathen, in perils in the city, in perils in the wilderness, in perils in the sea, in perils among false brethren; in weariness and painfulness, in watchings often, in hunger and thirst, in fastings often, in cold and nakedness. Besides those things that are without, that which cometh upon me daily, the care of all the churches. Who is weak, and I am not weak? who is offended, and I burn not?" (2 Cor. 11: 23-29)

The great Apostle had no disposition to ignore the fact of suffering and was too wise and too honest to pretend to dispose of suffering by denying its existence. He recognized the stubborn fact of affliction, "mortal flesh," and death as things real in the realm of the temporal; yet he did not stop with things temporal. He contended that things of the Spirit are equally real and more radiant.

I. THE GLORY OF THE TEMPORAL IS THAT IT REVEALS THE RADIANT REALITY OF THINGS THAT ARE SPIRITUAL AND TIMELESS

1. His reasoning reveals the perversity of the human mind in the two most prevalent attitudes man holds toward the material things of life. The most common sin of mankind is that of regarding the material things as the main things of life. This materialistic view and attitude toward life are and have ever been the prolific source of the major perils to real human progress. The second attitude is based upon negations, or a denial of the reality of anything material or temporal. Such attitude is not the result of any process of reasoning, but is rather a mental assumption without rhyme or reason. The theory seems to have a special appeal to human pride and the modern mania for short cuts and getting things easy. It has been reduced to a ritualistic formula: "If you desire a thing, you deserve it; go after what you want. If you meet with obstructions in your efforts to acquire, dispose of them. The best and quickest way to dispose of a foe is to deny its existence." Paul points out the futility of the first attitude and the fallacy of the other.

2. Paul is admonishing us to look through things temporal for deeper and richer truths. The carnally minded look to the temporal and get a drab and prosaic picture of life. The spiritually minded look through the temporal and get a kaleidoscopic view of the things of time and eternity.

As I sit at my desk hard by a window I look through the window pane and get a panoramic view of the beauties of nature. There to my left stands an orange tree with only a few golden ripe oranges dangling in the sunlight, reminding me of the harvest that was but is now steadily passing. Then on the same tree is a profusion of half-grown green oranges and even orange blossoms telling of a harvest that is yet to be. Above the window perched on the bough of a grapefruit tree sits a mother mocking-bird coaxing and caressing her fledgelings. I am hardly conscious of the intervening glass, as I look through upon a poem of nature set to rhythmic music by the singing birds. Then I turn to my text and am reminded that all these things are transitory, ephemeral, and temporal, and must be used exactly as I use the window pane in viewing eternal things. Day has passed, and night comes on. I look through the same window pane and fail to see a tree or a flower. I know they are there, but I must wait for the light of a new day to see them. I look up through the darkness and behold the heavens adorned and bedecked with fiery constellations. It seems to me that there are stars everywhere. Yet the astronomers tell me that the naked eye is capable of seeing comparatively few of the fixed stars. They tell us that by looking through a telescope they are enabled to see stars innumerable, all in constant motion, swarming in space like bees about the hive. By the use of the spectroscope they tell us what the stars are made of and give proof that they contain the same chemical elements with which we are familiar here on earth. Even the stars belong to the things of time. Our text tells us that things temporal are God's telescope through which we get a glimpse of the radiant realities of the spiritual and eternal realm.

3. Here and elsewhere, Paul emphasizes the inconsistency of a Christian's looking to the things of time. In verse 18 he says: "While we look not at the things which are seen, but at the things which are not seen: for the things which are seen are temporal; but the things which are not seen are eternal." His adverb "while" has been interpreted "because of," which would convey the idea that, to the Christian, "affliction" is made "light" and "momentary" by, and only by his mental attitude. There is an element of truth in the idea for both saint and sinner, but it is not the meaning of the passage. It would be truer to the meaning of the text to translate "while" as "since." What he is really saying is: "Since we are Christians we look not upon things that are seen." The word "for," as is common in Paul's writings, introduces his reason or argument in defense of his contention. We would not do violence either to the spirit or meaning of the text by translating it: "Since we are Christians, we look not upon things that are seen, but upon things that are not seen, because the things that are seen are temporal, and the things that are not seen are eternal."

What we are saying is that Paul's statement is true and will remain true regardless of our mental attitude. The word "look" is the same word from which we get our word "scope" or "mark" in the sense of a fixed goal. The idea here advanced is re-enforced by Paul's admonition in Colossians 3: 1-3: "If ye then be risen with Christ, seek those things which are above, where Christ sitteth on the right hand of God. Set your affections on things above, not on things on the earth. For ye are dead, and your life is hid with Christ in God."

His argument is that the very fact one is a Christian is an all-sufficient reason why he should fix the affection of his heart, or lavish the love of his life upon things above. It is the only course consistent with the spirit and genius of Christianity. To turn the picture, it is as inconsistent for a Christian to chase and clamor for the trivial and transitory things of time, as it would be for one to have pockets sewed in his shroud.

II. THE RADIANT PERSONALITY OF GOD IS REVEALED THROUGH THINGS TEMPORAL

1. We would not delimit the wisdom and power of God by suggesting that it had to be so, that he had to march through the avenue of nature in order to establish the fact of his existence, or that nature gives an adequate revelation of God; but the fact remains that through nature the revelation is made sufficiently clear as to render a verdict of guilt against all who oppose his will, and that "without excuse." "For the invisible things of him from the creation of the world are clearly seen, being understood by the things that are made, even his eternal power and Godhead; so that they are without excuse" (Rom. 1: 20). "Paul does not here teach that it is the design of God, in revealing himself to men, to render their opposition inexcusable, but rather, since this revelation has been made, they have in fact no apology for their ignorance and neglect of God. Though the revelation of God in his works is sufficient to render men inexcusable,

it does not follow that it is sufficient to lead men blinded by sin to a saving knowledge of himself." (Hodge, on Romans.)

2. God has revealed not only the fact and majesty of his being in and through nature, but has also revealed his love through providential provisions. He made a covenant provision with Noah and through Noah to all mankind, "While the earth remaineth, seedtime and harvest, and cold and heat, and summer and winter, and day and night shall not cease" (Gen. 8: 22). Paul met the idolaters of Lystra and marshaled a most convincing argument, and made an eloquent appeal for them to turn to God, on the basis of this covenant promise. "Nevertheless he left not himself without witness, in that he did good, and gave us rain from heaven, and fruitful seasons, filling our hearts with food and gladness" (Acts 14: 17).

David incorporates the revelation of God, both in nature and providence, in the Nineteenth Psalm, verses 1-4: "The heavens declare the glory of God; and the firmament sheweth his handywork. Day unto day uttereth speech, and night unto night sheweth knowledge. There is no speech nor language, where their voice is not heard. Their line is gone out through all the earth, and their words to the end of the world. In them hath he set a tabernacle for the sun." Dr. B. H. Carroll says: "Thus all nature in us or external to us, and God's marvelous providence proclaim the knowledge of him." Thomas Paine, the atheist, admitted all this, and expressed his admiration for Addison's paraphrase of Psalm 19:

The spacious firmament on high,
With all the blue ethereal sky,
And spangled heavens, a shining frame,
Their great Original proclaim:
The unwearied sun, from day to day,
Does his Creator's power display,
And publishes to every land
The work of an Almighty hand.

Soon as the evening shades prevail,
The moon takes up the wondrous tale,
And nightly to the listening earth
Repeats the story of her birth;
While all the stars that round her burn,
And all the planets in their turn,
Confirm the tidings as they roll,
And spread the truth from pole to pole.

What though, in solemn silence all
Move round the dark, terrestrial ball?
What though no real voice nor sound
Amid their radiant orbs be found?
In reason's ear they all rejoice,
And utter forth a glorious voice,
Forever singing as they shine,
"The hand that made us is divine!"

3. Jesus Christ was, and is, the fullest and finest revelation and interpretation of God. Nature revealed the fact and power and majesty of his being, but it remained for Jesus Christ to reveal to man his great throbbing, compassionate heart of love. "And the Word was made flesh, and dwelt among us (and we beheld his glory, as of the only begotten of the Father,) full of grace and truth" (John 1: 14). That is exactly the revelation Paul is talking about in 2

Corinthians 4: 6: "For God, who commanded the light to shine out of darkness, hath shined in our hearts, to give the light of the knowledge of the glory of God in the face of Jesus Christ."

III. THROUGH THINGS TEMPORAL WE HAVE A REVELATION OF THE RADIANT PLANS AND PURPOSES OF THE FATHER

Paul takes up the matter of affliction, and weighs it, measures it, and reveals the purpose it serves in the life of a Christian.

1. He weighs affliction in the balances of just deserts and says, "It's light." He is not speaking as a superficial fanatic, but a saint seasoned in the school of suffering.

I dared to quote this passage to a mother and daughter, both of whom have suffered for years from what the physicians say is an incurable disease. I was anxious to observe their reaction. "Mother, Paul says our affliction is light." Her ready reply was a shout, not a sob: "Oh, yes, compared with what Christ has suffered for us, we haven't suffered at all." That was an effective sermon, preached by a saint who has been confined to her wheelchair for a dozen years.

2. He not only weighs affliction, but measures it and calmly declares, "It is but for a moment." Is Paul speaking hastily, or defiantly? Is he speaking to chide or to comfort? When we reflect that these words were spoken by a saint whose life was but a protracted death, one who constantly bore about in his body the dying of Jesus, and who stood in constant peril of death, then we can fully appreciate the spirit

of his message. Paul measures his words and carefully balances his sublime sentence, "light stands opposed to weight," and "momentary stands opposed to eternal."

3. Having weighed and measured affliction, he tells us the purpose of it all. Our afflictions work for us, yet we regard affliction as our foe working against us. Paul says, "not so." He speaks with the tremendous emphasis of personal experience. "Our affliction is working for us more and more exceedingly an eternal weight of glory."

When we consider the beneficent purpose of the Father in permitting affliction and compare the weight and duration of our suffering and sorrow here with the eternal weight of glory, we can almost shout with Paul, "I reckon the sufferings of this present time are not worthy to be compared with the glory which shall be revealed in us" (Rom. 8: 18).

4. Finally, Paul's picture of unseen realities scintillates with radiant splendor against the black background of suffering and sorrow. He had presented his body as a living sacrifice unto God, and now "bearing about in his body the dying of the Lord Jesus," he stands on the threshold of time with an ever-deepening "desire to depart and to be with Jesus."

Regardless of who wrote the Book of Hebrews, we see the soul of Paul photographed in that marvelous passage, Hebrews 12: 27: "And this word . . . signifieth the removing of those things that are shaken, as of things that are made, that those things which cannot be shaken may remain." Freely, but fairly translated, the passage is in perfect harmony with

Paul's teaching here. "Things are shaking to pieces. Let 'em shake. They are man-made anyhow, and they are shaking to pieces that the things which are unshakable might remain."

Henry van Dyke eloquently expressed the faith of the great Apostle when he said: "I am not an optimist; there's too much evil in the world and in me. Nor am I a pessimist; there's too much good in the world, and a God. I am rather, I suppose, a meliorist, believing God wills to make the world better, trying to do my bit to help, and wishing it were more."

Chapter 2

ADORNING THE DOCTRINE

That they may adorn the doctrine of God our Saviour in all things.—TITUS 2: 10b.

HERE is a stupendous, staggering assignment, a challenging charge, a titanic task that is humanly impossible to accomplish.

"Humanly impossible!" That reminds me that the outstanding inventions and great discoveries that bless humanity today are the results of human beings doing the "humanly impossible." "Humanly impossible!" That is what they told Franklin, when he started out to bridle and harness the electricity of the air. "Humanly impossible!" That is what they told Watt when he started his steam engine. "Humanly impossible!" That is what they told Marconi when he talked of wireless telegraphy; but he explored the realm of impossibility and brought forth the radio as an additional trophy. The Wright brothers dared to do the impossible and gave to the world the airplane.

"Adorn the doctrine of God." How can an ordinary man adorn the doctrine? He can't. And from a human view the task seems even more hopeless when we observe that Paul was not talking to ordinary nor to extraordinary men. He was talking to Christian slaves about an imperative duty and an imperial privilege. It is a duty and privilege to "adorn the doctrine."

I. HERE IS A PLAIN DUTY THAT CLASHES WITH THE SPIRIT OF THE MODERN AGE

1. In the first place, the modern man has no desire to adorn the doctrine of God. There is rather an evident disposition on the part of large numbers of modern Christians to dilute, or to despise, doctrine. As someone has said: "Definite doctrine has been whittled down in the name of religion, until all that is left is an indescribable agglomeration of pious nebulosities." The spirit of this age is pictured in 2 Timothy 4: 3, 4: "For the time will come when they will not endure sound doctrine; but after their own lusts shall they heap to themselves teachers, having itching ears; and they shall turn away their ears from the truth, and shall be turned unto fables."

2. It is evident that too many preachers have yielded to the modern clamor for pious platitudes and glittering generalities. Such preaching was wisely characterized by Whatley when he said:

> Many a meandering discourse one hears, in which the preacher aims at nothing, and . . . hits it.

Pope's lines, written two hundred years ago, were never given prominence in sermonic literature until recent times.

> For modes of faith
> Let graceless zealots fight;
> He can't be wrong
> Whose life is in the right.

This sentiment fits the spirit of the modern age, but it clashes with the spirit and letter of Christianity. As a philosophy it has been repudiated in every realm, except the realm of religion. We have never heard a statesman, not even a wise politician, quote the companion lines from the same author:

> For forms of government let fools contest;
> Whate'er is best administer'd is best.

3. The type of preaching from the pulpits is invariably and inevitably reflected in the character of worshipers in the pews. That is paying high tribute to the influence of the ministry, but we must not forget that it places upon us a tremendous responsibility. God pity the people when their preacher is a timeserver, or a man-pleaser! A finer day has never dawned for a plain, positive, and emphatic proclamation of gospel truths.

Doctor Gambrell said: "No coward has any right to be a preacher. If the preacher is afraid of anyone in his church, afraid to speak his mind or to do right, that man ought to pray himself out of that timid atmosphere, or he ought to resign and go where he is not afraid." Certainly he was correct. A cowardly, cringing, conscienceless time-serving preacher is a monumental monstrosity—"an abomination of desolation" in the pulpit, or out.

We need not expect the people to reach a higher character level in life than that of the preacher. A shiftless, shallow, superficial, easy-going church is an indictment against some preacher. When one speaks of a church as a "sleeping giant," it simply means that someone in the pulpit needs to be aroused and stirred to a higher sense of his responsibility. A drifting congregation, wafted by every contrary wind that blows, is evidence that some preacher has failed in the primary purpose of his ministry, as pointed out by Paul in Ephesians 4: 12-15: "For the perfecting of the saints, for the work of the ministry, for the edifying of the body of Christ: till we all come in the unity of the faith, and of the knowledge of the Son of God, unto a perfect man, unto the measure of the stature of the fulness of Christ: that we henceforth be no more children, tossed to and fro, and carried about with every wind of doctrine, by the sleight of men and cunning craftiness, whereby they lie in wait to deceive; but speaking the truth in love, may grow up into him in all things, which is the head, even Christ."

The highest tributes I have ever heard paid to preachers were words of praise meant primarily for churches, but which reflected the character of their pastors. One of the greatest missionary leaders, and wisest counselors the country has ever produced, said of the church of which he was a faithful member: "It is a haven of rest and comfort to me beyond all words; it is the best church I ever saw; the men and women in it stay by the supreme things for which a church exists; they refuse to be turned aside by inconsequential and secondary things." The name of the pastor is not mentioned but his character is reflected in the love and loyalty of his members. He is one of Paul's double-honor pastors. "Let the elders that rule well be counted worthy of double honour, especially they who labour in the word and doctrine" (1 Tim. 5: 17).

The mere fact that Dr. I. M. Haldeman was pastor of the First Baptist Church of New York City for fifty years is evidence of his sterling character qualities and of his marked ability as a preacher. He was also a prolific writer. But the highest tribute ever paid the great pastor was words of praise meant primarily for his church: "The First Baptist Church of New York," says a great Bible teacher, "is the best informed group of Christians, and better grounded in the great teachings of the Scriptures, than any other church in America." That is a high tribute to the church, but equally so to the dear pastor, who has finished his course and crossed over. It tells us that he took seriously Paul's charge in 2 Timothy 4: 1, 2: "I charge thee therefore before God, and the Lord Jesus Christ, who shall judge the quick and the dead at his appearing and his kingdom; preach the word; be instant in season, out of season; reprove, rebuke, exhort with all longsuffering and doctrine."

II. REGARDLESS OF THE SPIRIT OF THE TIMES, AND REGARDLESS OF DIFFICULTIES, OUR DUTY REMAINS

We are enjoined, admonished, yea, exhorted to "adorn the doctrine of God."

1. The very fact that we are enjoined to undertake such a task is assurance of final success. Impossible? That is what they shouted to Daniel Webster, at the dedication of Bunker Hill monument, when he appealed to the surging throngs: "Stand back, gentlemen,

stand back!" "Impossible, Mr. Webster, impossible!" was the reply. Webster stepped to the edge of the platform and said: "Impossible? Nothing is impossible on Bunker Hill!" The crowds rolled back like a mighty tidal wave. Surely, there is nothing that God would have us do that is impossible of accomplishment.

2. We must take the task seriously. He nowhere commands us to be successful, but does demand unqualified fidelity. "Be thou faithful unto death"—not until death, but unto death. Be faithful, if it kills you. And then what? He will take care of the results. "I'll give you a crown of life." If any person on earth ought to take his task seriously, it is the preacher. He has the biggest task and the most urgent task under heaven. He ought to and he can adorn the doctrine of things divine, by a deathless devotion to and an earnestness in his work.

Frank W. Boreham, in one of his scintillating essays, tells of meeting an actor on the train as they journeyed through England. Mr. Boreham, with eyes and ears always open for new ideas, turned to the actor and asked: "How do you account for the interest of the people in theatrical performances? Certainly we know that you are merely acting, and that there is nothing real about it. Yet people will turn from the realities of life to see you act out your fiction. How do you explain it? Our churches are often empty, when your theaters are filled."

"It is like this," said the actor. "We take fiction and act it out as if it were a living reality, and too often the preacher takes living realities and treats them as if they were mere fiction."

What an indictment! How can we trifle? The wonder deepens when we recall the seriousness of our God-given tasks: "Now then we are ambassadors for Christ, as though God did beseech you by us: we pray you in Christ's stead, be ye reconciled to God" (2 Cor. 5: 20). Spurgeon said that Baxter preached, every time he entered the pulpit,

> As he ne'er might preach again,
> As a dying man to dying men.

That is exactly the way every preacher ought to preach.

3. The "doctrine of God" is adorned wherever the full gospel is faithfully proclaimed. Every soul saved makes the doctrine of salvation by grace more attractive; every effort made to win the lost at home, and to carry the glad tidings across the seas, emphasizes the sincerity of our faith in the "gospel as the power of God unto salvation to every one that believeth."

III. HOW CAN MAN ADORN THE DOCTRINE OF GOD?

It seems impossible and indeed is impossible if it is left to us. But when God commands the impossible we must trust him to make it possible. He always makes good.

1. We can adorn the doctrine of regeneration—the new birth. "Ye must be born again." "Lord, how can I?" That's God's part of the program. "My beloved, as ye have always obeyed, . . . work out your own salvation with fear and trembling." "How can I . . . ?" But wait—"For it is God which worketh in

you both to will and to do of his good pleasure." Certainly regeneration is the doctrine of God and the work of God. Paul tells us exactly how we adorn this glorious doctrine. As Christians we must "Walk not after the flesh, but after the Spirit. For the law of the Spirit of life in Christ Jesus hath made me free from the law of sin and death. For what the law could not do, in that it was weak through the flesh, God sending his own Son in the likeness of sinful flesh, and for sin, condemned sin in the flesh: that the righteousness of the law might be fulfilled in us, who walk not after the flesh, but after the Spirit" (Romans 8: 2-4).

David opens his Psalm of praise by pointing out the pleasure and profit that come to man when he walks within the will of God: "Blessed is the man that walketh not in the counsel of the ungodly, nor standeth in the way of sinners, nor sitteth in the seat of the scornful. But his delight is in the law of the Lord; and in his law doth he meditate day and night. And he shall be like a tree planted by the rivers of water, that bringeth forth his fruit in his season; his leaf also shall not wither; and whatsoever he doeth shall prosper" (Psalm 1: 1-3).

Paul is talking about the beauty of the doctrine of regeneration in 2 Corinthians 3: 2, 3. "Ye are our epistle, written in our hearts, known and read of all men: . . . declared to be the epistle of Christ ministered by us, written not with ink, but with the spirit of the living God; not in tables of stone, but in fleshy tables of the heart." Regeneration, or the new birth, is the most spiritual of spiritual matters. It means Christianity written in the heart. Christianity written in the human heart is Christianity in its most legible form; Christianity written in the human heart is Christianity in its most persuasive form; and Christianity written in the human heart is Christianity in its most enduring form. Unbelievers do not read our Bible, but they read us.

Christ, in Matthew 5: 16, is telling us how we may make attractive the doctrine of the new life, "Let your light so shine before men, that they may see," —you? No,—"your good works, and glorify your Father which is in heaven." That person who so lives as to cause others to glorify God is surely making every work of grace more attractive.

2. It is possible for us to adorn the doctrine of divine providence. God has made providential provision for every life. His plan is not only the best plan, but the only plan that promises peace and success. By renouncing our own plan and accepting his plan for life, we say to all the world: "He is all wise, and therefore he knows what is best for us; and since he loves us with an infinite love, he must choose the best possible plan for our lives; and since he is all powerful, he is able to see us through if, and when, we accept his plan."

There are some things that we could never know in a vital sense without personally experiencing them or by observing them in the life of another. I recall quite distinctly when my attention was first called to the word "providence." To me it was just another big word without meaning; and explanations failed to explain, until my dear old pastor took me into his confidence and permitted me to witness how the purposes and plans of God had unfolded in his life. He taught me the fine art of yielding to God's will.

> Would you in His Kingdom find a place of constant rest?
> Would you prove Him true in providential test?
> Would you in His service labor always at your best?
> Let Him have His way with thee.

3. Finally, we adorn the doctrine of God's boundless, comforting grace when we show the right spirit of fortitude in the hour of sorrow.

Sometime since, news came to me of the great sorrow that had befallen my good friend and former teacher in the sudden and tragic death of a fine son. I recalled how faithfully the old teacher had given himself to the task of teaching young preachers how to preach the gospel of comforting grace to other hurting hearts. I wondered if he would be able to stand the strain of the crushing blow. I hastened to write to him, giving assurance of my prayerful sympathy. In due time an answer came which allayed every fear, and did more. My former teacher made the doctrine of comforting grace plainer and more beautiful in the crucial hour of life than he had ever done in the classroom. He sent the following simple lines which gave me a glimpse of a brave heart, standing in the dark, holding on to God.

> I want to let go, but I won't let go,
> There are battles to fight;
> By day and by night for God and the right,
> And I'll never let go.

RADIANT REALITIES

I want to let go, but I won't let go,
I'm sick 'tis true;
Worried and blue, and worn through and through,
But I won't let go.

I want to let go, but I won't let go,
I will never yield;
What, lie down on the field and surrender my shield,
No! I'll never let go.

I want to let go, but I won't let go,
May this be my song, 'mid legions of wrong;
Oh, God, keep me strong,
That I may never let go.

—*Anonymous.*

Chapter 3

A DISSOLVER OF DOUBT

And I have heard of thee, that thou canst . . . dissolve doubts.—DANIEL 5: 16a.

THERE are two distinct types of doubt, and each type has its own source.

First, there is such a thing as honest doubt, growing out of intellectual difficulties. These difficulties may relate to the field of science, or they may grow out of false deductions from providential dispensations.

Horace Bushnell says: "Science puts everything in question, and literature distils the questions, making an atmosphere of them." Tennyson speaks of the "sunnier side of doubt." He certainly does not mean that there is anything bright or cheerful about doubt. The only ground for cheer in our doubts is the fact that we are capable of doubting at all. It means that we are more than animals. Birds and beasts are guided by intuition and instinct; but we are created in the image of God, capable of reasoning and reaching intelligent conclusions. Therefore, we are invited to "come . . . and let us reason together." Thoreau says: "If I could not doubt, I should not believe." Then the possibility of doubt is the price we must pay for the privilege of being more than animals. It is our privilege to investigate and acquire knowledge, and no person is made to doubt because of superior knowledge or high discovery.

Then there is such a thing as honest doubt growing out of deep concern, or moral earnestness. A person who is too superficial to think deeply and too indifferent really to care would hardly doubt. That is the type Cowper speaks of when he says:

> He who never doubted of his state,
> He may, perhaps, perhaps he may, too late.

Second, there is such a thing as dishonest doubt. Doubt that takes root in and springs from immoral conduct is as dishonest as it is dishonorable. If it were possible for some discerning statistician to get at the facts and record his findings, I suspect we would discover that most of our doubts are based upon low living rather than upon a lack of knowledge. Regardless of their bases, Pascal points out the wise way for us to deal with them: "To doubt is a misfortune, but to seek when in doubt is an indispensable duty. So he who doubts and seeks not is at once unfortunate and unfair."

It was a high tribute the pleasure-loving queen and godless king paid Daniel in the day of their doubts. The kingdom was failing and the king was frantic. He turned to Daniel as the Doubt Dissolver. Oh, how this war-torn, wicked, and reckless world needs the Daniel type today. Every preacher ought to be a dissolver of doubts wherever he goes. It is the high privilege of every Christian to live so as to cause doubts in the lives of friends to dissolve and disappear even as gulf clouds are driven before the morning sun. How does the world about us look upon us? It is a misfortune to doubt, but there are some things worse than honest doubt.

I. THERE IS SUCH A THING AS GENERATING AND DEVELOPING DOUBT IN THE HEARTS OF OTHERS

There are those who sow seeds of suspicion and skepticism with both hands.

1. The cynical spirit creates discord and doubt wherever he goes. I was somewhat surprised when I first discovered that our words "cynic" and "dog" come from the same Greek word. But upon a closer observation of the characteristics of both I detect a striking similarity. The cynic, like a dog, snarls and snaps at everything in sight. Paul had the cynic in mind when he said: "Beware of dogs" (Phil. 2: 3). Ferrar Fenton translates it; "Beware of the cynics." He generally poses as an iconoclast pretending to make battle against sham. In reality, he himself is a sham and will assassinate the character of a saint who stands in the way of the realization of his selfish plans. His conduct is determined by a false and dangerous philosophy of life. He assumes that he must pull others down in order to make room for his own promotion. He plays down and talks down everyone except himself. The cynical spirit has left a trail of gloom and destruction from Diogenes down to Clarence Darrow, who admonished college graduates to junk their diplomas and commit suicide.

The cynic is a destructionist in any field, but in

the field of religion he is more diabolical because there is more involved. A cynical preacher is the greatest curse in Christendom. He is always on a parade posing as a paragon of wisdom and piety. He feels that he must assassinate the character of all other preachers in order to attract public attention to himself. He reminds us of Tennyson's "foul bird of rapine whose prey is man's good name." He implants suspicion and develops doubt in the minds of all who come under his influence. He bemoans and bewails the fact that all others have sold out to the enemy, dipped their colors to the foe, or, are controlled by some imaginary machine and, lo, he alone is left to save the world. Emerson has a message for such preachers: "Don't hang a dismal picture on the wall, and do not daub with sables and glooms in your conversations. Don't be a cynical and disconsolate preacher. Don't bewail and bemoan. Omit the negative propositions. Nerve us with incessant affirmatives."

2. The teacher is often guilty of generating doubt in the minds of the young. He raises captious questions and, as Bushnell says, "distils them into an atmosphere."

A physician told me of an old professor in a great medical school which is notorious for the number of agnostics, atheists, and infidels that have come from her lecture halls. The old professor would take his final fling at whatever faith survived the four-year course by the interrogative statement: "Now, young gentlemen, you have studied the anatomy of man from head to foot. You have studied the functions of every organ, scrutinized every bone, muscle, and nerve cell. Have you discovered anything that corresponds to what the preacher calls the soul?" One of the profane students of this same old professor was telling a pious old Negro about dissecting human bodies from the tip of the toes to the crown of the head, and how he had sought for and failed to find any trace of the soul. The old Negro made a wise reply: "The Lord bless yo heart, honey—looking for a soul in a dead man."

3. Every immoral person generates gloom and doubt for all about him. David tells us, in the Seventy-third Psalm, how he almost slipped and nearly lost his footing under the influence of ungodly arrogance. "Almost slipped"—not altogether—"nearly"; yet the grace of God saved him, and he rails with righteous indignation against all ungodliness that would make a man behave like a beastly brute.

But when bad influences emanate from the lives of professed Christians, as is often the case, the havoc wrought is unspeakably worse. A professed Christian who is careless in his conduct compromises the idealism of his church and brings reproach upon the causes dear to the heart of Christ.

II. THERE ARE OTHERS WHO MAY BE CALLED DOUBT DISPENSERS

They may not be classified as doubters themselves, but they make it easy for others to come under the influence of doubt.

1. They do not start doubt, they spread it. They take pleasure in relating how and when faith was as-

saulted by agnosticism, defeated by infidelity, or slaughtered by the skeptic. They arrange for the debate and provide a congregation for atheists who cannot get a hearing on their own merit.

2. They do not intentionally plant doubt in any heart, they merely propagate it. They reproduce the age-old harangue of dead infidels. As Spurgeon puts it, they give to the living "a dish of dead men's brains."

I recall a very pathetic incident in an early pastorate which points out the danger of such a course. A strong man with a wife and three children had lived within five blocks of our church for several years, and not a member of the family had ever attended public worship. The mother was sick and the children were being neglected. The case was presented to the church and some of our good women went out and cleaned the house and carried fresh linen and food, as Christians should have done. I followed up their work and tried to tell the story of God's love, but the story was scorned. Finally, the father came to see the pastor. He had a haggard expression on his face.

"Sir," he said, "my wife told me of your visit yesterday, and how you read and prayed for us. I have come to ask you if you will try again. My wife is dying and I want you to go and tell her how to die."

"Have you talked to her, and does she know of the seriousness of her case?" I asked.

"She knows she can't live, but I can't talk to her. You don't understand," he continued. "When we were married she was attending the little church with her father and mother, who were good Christians. I have talked infidelity in the home and pretended not to believe in churches and Christians. I see my mistake, but now she is harder than I am."

He was greatly disturbed, and I wanted to help him.

"You have assigned to me a difficult task," I said, "but since you have made this honest confession to me, I want you to help me by being just as honest with her."

He eagerly asked: "What can I do?"

"You owe it to yourself and to your family to make the same frank confession to them that you have made to me. I want you to go home and make that confession and ask her to forgive you."

It was a hard assignment for him, but he did it. I waited for him to finish his story before entering the home. The clouds had lifted, my task was easy and glorious. I asked for the little Testament I had read from and left with her on the day before. She handed it to me opened at John 3: 16. I read some promises and offered prayer for her and the home, then quoted the old song:

> Come, ye sinners, poor and needy,
> Weak and wounded, sick and sore;
> Jesus ready stands to save you,
> Full of pity, love and pow'r.
>
> I will arise and go to Jesus,
> He will embrace me in His arms;
> In the arms of my dear Saviour,
> Oh, there are ten thousand charms.

Her doubts were dissolved and she was ready to go home when the death angel came two days later.

III. THEN, THERE ARE DOUBT DISSOLVERS

Just as there are characters who create and dispense doubts, there are others whose conduct and character will dissolve, dispel, and sound the deathknell to doubts.

1. Daniel was such a character. Like the Master, he was true to the highest and best. There was nothing cunning, nor subtle, nor devious about his character or his teaching. Note how he talks to the king. He knew that licentious living, even back to the days of the king's father, was the fertile source of his doubts.

"O thou king, the most high God gave Nebuchadnezzar thy father a kingdom, and majesty, and glory, and honour. . . . But when his heart was lifted up, and his mind hardened in pride, he was deposed from his kingly throne, and they took his glory from him. . . . And thou, his son, O Belshazzar, hast not humbled thine heart, though thou knewest all this; but hast lifted up thyself against the Lord of heaven; . . . and thou hast praised the gods of silver, and gold, of brass, iron, wood and stone, which see not, nor hear, nor know: and the God in whose hand thy breath is, and whose are all thy ways, hast thou not glorified" (Daniel 5: 18-23).

2. Again, Daniel though brave as a lion, yet like the Master, was very tender.

Two of the tenderest incidents recorded in the New Testament are those of Jesus dealing with the doubts of John the Baptist and Thomas. The case of John the Baptist seems to bear out the contention that doubt in the realm of the Spirit, like cancer in the physical realm, is often caused by some crushing blow. John was in prison because of his deep love and daring fidelity to his Lord. Now he knew that Jesus was just over the hill in another city. He believed that Jesus had the power to release him from his prison cell. He wondered why he didn't come to him. He doubted, but was manifestly fair and wise in dealing with his doubts. He went to the right source for the truth. He sent two disciples to Jesus with the plain pointed question: "Art thou the Christ, or shall we look for another?" It seems that Jesus called John's disciples closer to him, and then performed miracle after miracle and sent them away with more than a verbal reply, yea, with a fresh personal experience. "Go tell John what you have seen and heard."

Again, it seems that the case of Thomas bears witness to the contention of Tennyson, that doubts are indicative of thinking and feeling deeply.

Thomas was not with the other disciples when Jesus appeared. But the fact of his appearance was reported to Thomas by his own comrades who were eye-witnesses. Yet Thomas doubted, and seems almost cruel in the conditions he imposes to dispel his doubts, and make it possible for him to believe. Jesus knew all about his dark and stubborn doubts, and was as tender as a mother in dissolving them. It seems that he appeared a second time for Thomas' benefit. "Thomas, reach forth thy fingers; put them in the nail prints and thrust thy hand into my side, be not faithless, but believing." Thomas' doubt dissolved and he exclaimed: "My Lord and my God."

3. But not all the doubt dissolvers lived in the old days. Most of us have touched elbows with and have come under the beneficent influence of such characters.

I recall with increasing joy and gratitude some great and good Christian characters with whom I came in close contact in early life. My life has been richer, fuller, deeper, and sweeter since I sat at their feet. I gladly pay tribute to my "father in the ministry," Elder J. H. Grime, now living at Lebanon, Tennessee, and growing old gracefully. I came under the influence of his ministry just when the devil was doing his utmost to down me and destroy me with doubts. My doubts centered in myself, but at times I doubted the justice of God in thwarting my plans, and his wisdom in wanting me to be a preacher. Doubting was easy, believing was difficult. But the very presence of Brother Grime would cause my doubts to dissolve and start a song in my heart. I am sending him a copy of this sermon as a belated tribute of gratitude. He will remember how he advised me to go to Baylor University, primarily for the privilege of sitting at the feet of Dr. B. H. Carroll in Bible study.

I sat at the feet and looked into the face of Doctor Carroll for five years. The best-marked volumes in my library are the books written by my great teacher. He was truly great from every viewpoint—great in physique, great in intellect, great in heart, and greater in faith. He himself was once a doubter, but through the grace of God he became one of the greatest doubt dissolvers the South has ever known.

Then there was Dr. J. B. Gambrell, to whom I am indebted beyond words to acknowledge. As a youthful pastor he was my beau ideal. He gave me my first lesson in writing and conducted his last revival meeting in a church of which I was pastor. The very memory of his ministry is like a breath from heaven. As often as I think of him I am reminded of Froude's tribute to Victor Hugo. "I cannot," says Froude, "bring myself to believe that Hugo ever had a sorry thought, even in the dark." There are hundreds of us who feel exactly that way about Doctor Gambrell. His great life radiated spiritual light that destroyed doubt even as sunshine destroys germs.

Michael Faraday, the Edison of England in the nineteenth century, was dying. Sir Humphrey Davy discovered Faraday and declared him to be his greatest discovery. His life and exploits in the field of science were scrutinized by a dozen biographers, all of whom agreed at least on one point—that: "Michael Faraday was the most transparently honest soul that the realm of science ever produced." The world knew him as a great scientist, his friends knew him as a great Christian. Reporters rushed to his bedside for a final interview. They well knew that the waiting world would want to know how the great scientist would face death.

"What are your speculations?" they inquired. "Speculations?" he asked in tones of wondering surprise. "Speculations! I have none! I am resting on certainties. 'I know whom I have believed, and am persuaded that he is able to keep that which I have committed unto him against that day.'" So the great

RADIANT REALITIES

Christian and scientist dissolved doubts by his noble life and by his confirmed faith even in death.

I have closed the door on DOUBT,
I will go by what light I can find,
And hold up my hands and reach them out
To the glimmer of God in the dark, and call–
"I am Thine, though I grope and stumble and fall,
I serve, and Thy service is kind."

I have closed the door on FEAR.
He has lived with me far too long.
If he were to break forth and reappear,
I should lift up my eyes and look at the sky,
And sing aloud, and run lightly by;
He will never follow a song.

I have closed the door on GLOOM.
His house has too narrow a view;
I must seek for my soul a wider room
With windows to open and let in the sun,
And radiant lamps when the day is done,
And the breeze of the world blowing through.*
–*Irene McKeehan.*

* From *1000 Quotable Poems.* By permission Willett, Clark & Co., Chicago.

Chapter 4

DAVID'S RECIPE FOR HAPPINESS

> Fret not thyself because of evildoers, neither be thou envious against the workers of iniquity. For they shall soon be cut down like the grass, and wither as the green herb. Trust in the Lord, and do good; so shalt thou dwell in the land, and verily thou shalt be fed. Delight thyself also in the Lord; and he shall give thee the desires of thine heart. Commit thy way unto the Lord; trust also in him; and he shall bring it to pass. And he shall bring forth thy righteousness as the light, and thy judgment as the noonday. Rest in the Lord, and wait patiently for him; fret not thyself because of him who prospereth in his way, because of the man who bringeth wicked devices to pass.—PSALM 37: 1-7.

C. H. SPURGEON said a good introduction to a sermon is like an attractive porch to a handsome home. It gives a pleasing approach to the premises. But we are not visiting a home today, we are going to Doctor David's clinic. He is a skilled diagnostician and a specialist in treating a common aggravated form of heart trouble, the symptoms of which are melancholy, fits of dispondency, and general debility. The disease is aggravated by the patient's fretting and fuming, mostly about nothing. His remedy has never failed to produce a permanent cure for any patient who has faithfully applied it.

Like most good physicians, Doctor David begins with a negative, which is the most difficult part of any prescription. But it is always so; regardless of what ails you, there *is* something you must quit, something you must give up before you can get well. Like it or not, if we would be strong, vigorous, useful, and happy, we must apply the remedy. Here it is:

I. QUIT YOUR FRETTING. "Fret not thyself."

1. Why not quit it? It doesn't help you, nor does it enable you to help others.

Dr. J. B. Gambrell gave me this sermon and illustrated it by the life he lived. The last series of evangelistic sermons he ever preached was in a small-town church on the plains of Texas, where it was my privilege to be pastor. Doctor Gambrell read these seven verses from the Thirty-seventh Psalm in our family devotional around the breakfast table. For some reason, perhaps for my personal benefit, he read the same passage two mornings. Each morning he closed the book, and with that quaint characteristic twinkle in his eye, and with a soft and soothing tone he said: "We need that. It is one of my favorite Psalms." In one of the morning services he used the same passage, and gave us a message that made some of us over. He told the story of an old man. He didn't tell his name, but some of us guessed it. The old man was coming into Fort Worth from the West, and was anxious about making connection with a train for Dallas. For some reason the train stopped out on the prairie. The passengers began to raise the windows and look down toward the engine. Soon all the men were out on the ground, most of them murmuring and complaining, but it didn't seem to help the situation. The old man passed the time profitably reading his New Testament and humming snatches of great old hymns. Finally, a handsome lady (Doctor Gambrell said she was put up like a Presbyterian, but did not explain it) who had possessed her soul in patience as long as she could, began to look at her watch, wring her hands and prance up and down the aisle of the coach. She stood directly before the old man, who sat with calm, poise, and patience, humming his song: "Why, pray tell me, why do they insist on staying out here in the country? I must get to Fort Worth. Why don't they go on?" The old man looked up and smiled and said: "Lady, this train doesn't run on the steam that you get up." Oh, if the lady got the lesson, it was doubtless worth all that it cost and more.

When I was a lad I took up the study of palmistry. They made me believe that I could read character by the lines in the palm of the hand. I discovered a better way than that and quit palmistry and started preaching. Palmistry told me that all those little criss-cross lines and crow's-feet in the palm of the hand were caused by fretting. Fretting will do worse than making cross lines in the hand; it will make you cross in the home and everywhere. If it never helps and always hinders, why not quit it?

2. A good sober view reveals that for a Christian fretting is not only sinful, it is silly. Most of us have been guilty, if we are not guilty now. We burn blood, burst nerve cells, waste energy, and sometimes wreck health in useless fretting.

The finest bit of philosophy I have ever heard on the subject was given by Dr. B. H. Carroll, the great preacher and teacher of Texas. He told his Bible class the story of how his father enforced the lesson of the folly of fretting. Doctor Carroll's father was a big man, physically and otherwise. He had a large family of strong and stalwart sons. It was his custom to assign a task to the boys at the beginning of each week. He would assign a task and say: "Now, boys, you can finish this work by Saturday night. If you will work hard you can finish it by Friday night. If you get through Friday you may take Saturday off for any legitimate play or recreation." Doctor Carroll said that as surely as they worked hard and had a day for play, it seemed, to the young Carrolls, that the very elements conspired against them. It would rain, or snow and turn cold and keep them indoors. There they would be, murmuring and complaining. But the wise old father soon put a stop to their fretting. He called them together and said, "Now, boys, you must stop your fretting and complaining. I give you permission to fret and fume about anything and everything on earth except two things: *You are not to fret about that you can help.* You are able-bodied men; if you can help a situation it is your duty to do it and not waste your time fretting about it. And you are not to fret about anything you *can't help.* If you can't help it, fretting is not going to do any good but will do you harm." That is real philosophy. If you can help your situation, quit fretting and address yourself to the task; if you can't help it, it is silly to fret about it.

Let us leave the negative and turn to the positive. We need the tonic of what Emerson called "incessant affirmatives." David prescribes them.

II. "TRUST IN THE LORD AND DO GOOD"

Why not trust him? He has never failed a human heart.

1. Surely we can trust his love. His marvelous, matchless love for us is a guarantee that he will do his best, for "God commendeth his love toward us, in that, while we were yet sinners, Christ died for us" (Romans 5: 8).

> How the tho't enthralls me
> That whate'er befalls me,
> One will always love me the same;
> Not a trial ever causes Him to sever
> From the ones who honor His name.
>
> He will keep His promise to me,
> All the way with me He will go;
> He has never broken any promise spoken;
> He will keep His promise, I know.*
>
> —*Henry P. Morton.*

2. We can trust his wisdom. We cannot trust the wisdom of man. We are seldom ever certain as to the things we want most, and never certain as to what is best for us. But since he is infinitely wise we can trust his wisdom.

> I know my heav'nly Father knows
> The balm I need to soothe my woes,
> And with his touch of love divine,
> He heals this wounded soul of mine.

* By permission Robert H. Coleman, Dallas, Texas.

3. We can trust his power. He, who spoke the world into existence and created man in his own image, certainly has power to fulfil his purposes of love and wisdom. We can trust him with unwavering confidence. He loved us and died for us, and has wisdom and power to provide for us. And that is exactly what he promises to do. "So shalt thou dwell in the land, and verily thou shalt be fed."

David is declaring that the person who trusts in the Lord and does what good he can do shall surely dwell in the land and shall not starve to death. Some have imagined that they have discovered a false note in David's positive promise. We have known many to beg bread, but we did not know that they were "his seed." David puts it much stronger in verse 25: "I have been young, and now am old; yet have I not seen the righteous forsaken, nor his seed begging bread."

III. "DELIGHT THYSELF ALSO IN THE LORD"

This simply means that we are to look to the Lord for the deeper, finer, and abiding joys of life.

1. Those who look to the things of this world for joy will meet with disappointment. There is such a thing as worldly pleasure, but it is trivial, transitory, ephemeral. The cup of pleasure the world proffers has the bitterness of gall and the dregs of death in its depths.

2. But look to the Lord for the finer, richer, deeper, and sweeter joys of life and verily thou shalt not be disappointed. The devil promises much, but is a

poor payer. The Lord promises much and gives more than he promises.

3. The person who delights himself in the Lord will desire the right things and the Lord will want him to have them. "And he shall give thee the desires of thine heart."

IV. "COMMIT THY WAY UNTO THE LORD"

Literally, this means that I am to roll the whole burden of life upon the shoulders of God.

1. "Commit thy way" means more than merely to commend and to praise God. It means an unconditional surrender of your will and ways to the will of God. You can't manage your life independently of him. The threads of life are hopelessly entangled; you can't straighten them out. Life's problems are too perplexing, too intricate, and for all your struggling you will not be able to solve them. The Lord knows all about the frailty of man. He witnesses our futile efforts and seems to say: "Roll your burdens upon my shoulders; I care for you, and I can bear them. Leave all of life's problems with me; I know the solution for each and all; put the reins of life over in my hands, I know the way; I am the way and will bring it to pass." He is watching, waiting, and listening for each of us to say:

> Have Thine own way, Lord! have Thine own way!
> Hold o'er my being absolute sway!
> Fill with Thy Spirit, till all shall see
> Christ only, always, living in me!

2. The very thing the Psalmist is talking about is beautifully illustrated in a story related by Henry

Drummond. He was visiting a friend in the hills of Scotland. When the day for his departure came, his host told him the pathetic story of his teamster and coachman, who was a graduate of a leading university and famed as a skilled horseman, but who had fallen victim to strong drink. The host arranged for Mr. Drummond to make the journey to the station with the coachman alone, hoping that he might be of help to him. He asked permission to sit with the driver, which was granted, of course. As they drove leisurely through the mountains, the great preacher did his best to win a soul and save a life for Kingdom service. Time after time he had his man, as he hoped, at the very door of decision, but each time he refused to enter on the plea of the frailty of the flesh. "I can't," he would say, "I have tried to break away, but I'm too weak." Finally the preacher turned and said: "Suppose as we drive through these mountain roads, with rocky crags and deep cliffs at every turn, that your horses should become frightened and you should lose control and our lives were endangered, but you knew that I was a master in managing horses, and that I was waiting for you to put the lines in my hands, what would you do?" Timing his words to his actions, he turned and said: "I would give you the reins." That is a picture of what Christ would have us do, and he stands ready to take the reins of life.

V. "REST IN THE LORD, AND WAIT PATIENTLY FOR HIM"

The soul's one and only hope for rest, real, constant, abiding rest, is in him.

1. That is what Jesus promises in Matthew 11: 28,

"Come unto me, all ye that labour and are heavy laden, and I will give you rest." The literal translation reads: "I will rest you." Sin is the cause of all unrest, the poison which has fevered every life, the root of all weakness and weariness. Rest is the one thing for which the soul sighs, and the heart hungers.

The poet pictures the plight of every soul in its struggle with sin:

> Trust me nor fortunes, the poet feigns
> Can match the fierce unutterable pains
> Of him who, day and night,
> Devoid of rest,
> Carries his own accuser
> In his breast.

Rest is something that man cannot earn by his efforts, nor secure by his struggling, nor purchase as a reward of labor, nor capture as a price of pursuit. It is a gift of God. We find it "in Christ." Jesus speaks of his peace which the world can neither give nor take away.

We are enjoined to commit to Christ the whole question of sin, and to rest the soul's case with him. That is what Paul tells us he did. "I know whom I have believed, and am persuaded that he is able to keep that which I have committed unto him against that day" (2 Tim. 2: 12).

2. The rest we find in Christ means more than physical relaxation. He does not promise a release from labor, rest from toil, or a life of ease. "Take my yoke upon you." But, as Matthew Henry points out, "The yoke is lined with love." The "yoke" signifies

service, but there is joy and rest in it. We do not rest from toil, but find rest in toil.

Henry Drummond tells the story of two painters, each of whom painted a picture to illustrate his conception of rest. The first chose for his scene a quiet, still lake far back in the mountains. The second put on the canvas a plunging, thundering waterfall, with a fragile birch tree bending and dipping its branches in its foam. At the fork of a branch a robin sat quietly and calmly on its nest. "The first," says Drummond, "was stagnation, the last was rest."

3. "Rest in the Lord." That is the only hope for the suffering and sorrowing and overburdened. David tells us what to do with our burdens: "Cast thy burden upon the Lord, and he shall sustain thee" (Psalm 55: 22). Peter gives like counsel in 1 Peter 5: 7: "Casting all your care upon him, for he careth for you."

But observe, we must cast our burdens and sorrows upon him, commit them to him, and rest the whole matter in his hands. Too many of us take our burdens, and sometimes make them heavier by parading them and using them as a sort of an appeal for sympathy. We take our cares, our anxieties, our trials and troubles to the Lord and spread them out before him with a plea—"Lord, are you not sorry for poor little me?" Then we gather them all up and bear them back home. We will have another parade tomorrow. That is exactly what we are not to do with our troubles; not parade them, but place them in his hands, commit them, one and all, to the Lord.

The old negro has tried to sing it into our hearts.

RADIANT REALITIES

When your enemies assail, and your heart begins to fail,
Don't forget that God in heaven answers prayer;
He will make a way for you and will lead you safely thro';
Take your burden to the Lord and leave it there.

Leave it there, leave it there,
Take your burden to the Lord and leave it there;
If you trust and never doubt,
He will surely bring you out;
Take your burden to the Lord and leave it there.

If your body suffers pain, and your health you can't regain,
And your soul is almost sinking in despair,
Jesus knows the pain you feel, He can save and He can heal;
Take your burden to the Lord and leave it there.

Chapter 5

THE PURPOSE OF PRAYER

And it came to pass, that, as he was praying in a certain place, when he ceased, one of his disciples said unto him, Lord, teach us to pray, as John also taught his disciples. —LUKE 11: 1.

Therefore I say unto you, What things soever ye desire, when ye pray, believe that ye receive them, and ye shall have them. And when ye stand praying, forgive, if ye have ought against any: that your Father also which is in heaven may forgive you your trespasses. But if ye do not forgive, neither will your Father which is in heaven forgive your trespasses.—MARK 11: 24-26.

PRAYER occupies a prominent place in the Bible. Jesus said ten times as much about praying as he said about preaching. That is not saying that Jesus depreciated preaching, but does suggest a deeper appreciation of prayer. The popular idea is that prayer is a very simple matter. In reality it is the highest exercise of the soul and requires for its presentation the highest powers of the soul. Jesus nowhere tries to make prayer appear easy, but does make it attractive by the very earnestness of his appeals and admonitions. In the sixth chapter of Matthew he assumes that every Christian will do two things: first, that a Christian will do some giving; and second, that a Christian will do some praying. He does not assume that we will do as much of either as we ought to do, nor that we will do either as we ought. In his teaching he lifts giving and praying to a higher spiritual plane.

If you are a Christian you will do some praying, whether you are strong or weak, learned or illiterate, enlisted or idle. The question arises, why do you pray? Perhaps the weak and idle and ignorant would give one answer, while the strong and wise and useful would give quite another.

I. WHAT IS THE PURPOSE OF PRAYER?

1. There are those who tell us that the sole virtue in prayer is in its reflex influence. It does us good, they tell us, to humble ourselves in recognition of our utter dependence upon some force outside of and beyond us. But unless we recognize that the mysterious Force, whether we name it or not, is a living personality who knows our needs and is capable of making himself known to us and of supplying our needs, then we might as well humble ourselves before the gods of the heathen.

Such prayers, if indeed they can be called prayers at all, are offered by those who have a wrong conception of God. They either do not believe in a personal God, or else they do not believe that the omnipotent, omniscient, and omnipresent God is concerned about the individual. They argue that it is absurd to suppose that a mere wish or desire expressed in prayer should cause any deviation in the fixed order of the universe, for infinite wisdom which foresees all to take orders from a suppliant who foresees nothing. These peculiar ideas possess a certain order of mind, from which source comes the modern question, Can an intelligent person believe in prayer? It is a strange question, in view of the fact that intelligent people have believed in everything else from ghostly voices of spiritualist mediums to the vagaries of so-called Christian science. Still it remains that intelligent people do pray and give eloquent testimony to the fact that a loving Father hears and answers prayer.

But why do you pray?

2. The answer comes from another group, certainly more devout, if less thoughtful: "We pray because we feel that we must tell the Father our needs and desires,"—to be pointed, to inform God. But he knoweth all about our needs even before we ask him. One of the chiefest incentives to prayer is a consciousness of the fact that our Father knows all about our needs and desires. He has the hairs of our heads numbered and knows even our secret, unexpressed thoughts. No, we do not pray to inform God. He knoweth what is in man, and needeth not that any should tell him. Then, why do we pray?

3. Still others reply: "We pray to move God to change his attitude toward us." That is a more common and a more grievous error, because it reflects on the character of God. I am sorry to say that this idea is being encouraged in large Christian circles. I am confident that the hurtful error grows out of a misinterpretation of two parables: "The friend at midnight," recorded in Luke 11: 6-13, and "the importunate widow and the unjust judge," Luke 18: 1-8. Surely no thoughtful Christian would think of the hardhearted neighbor, who helped his neighbor in the

hour of need just to get rid of him, as a representative of God. It would be even worse to make the unjust judge represent God. He feared not God nor regarded man, but gave aid to the defenseless widow because he was afraid that she would give him a black eye. The very reverse is true in both instances. The force of the argument marshaled by our Lord from these parables is in the unlikeness of God to the heartless neighbor and unjust judge. But if we make the neighbor who pleaded for bread with importunity, and likewise the widow, represent the true Christian suppliant, the inference is so clear as to be tantamount to an assertion that we must move God the Father to change his mind, or his attitude, toward us. This is nowhere revealed more forcefully than in what I would call a staged fast.

When the late Dr. F. C. McConnell was pastor of the First Baptist Church of Waco, Texas, the church invited a rather superficial, eccentric evangelist to assist in a series of evangelistic services. The meeting was lacking the emotional enthusiasm the evangelist desired. In reality it was lacking in spiritual power. The pastor was lamenting that fact and pleading with his people to be much in prayer, when the evangelist jumped upon the platform and asked: "How many will join me in spending the night here in fasting and praying?" Not a hand was lifted. Then the pastor responded, "No, we will not stay here all night. We will get down on our knees and ask his blessing upon the meeting, and pray for such a deep spiritual concern for souls that will drive sleep from our eyes and then we will go home." I heard a whispered word of criticism of the great pastor. But he was exactly right. A staged fast might have some psychological effect upon a community, and it may have publicity value in attracting the curious, but is anti-scriptural.

No, we do not pray to move God, to change his attitude toward us. He does not need to change. Very likely we need to change our attitude toward right and wrong; but his attitude is right, and how grateful we ought to be that he is unchangeable! He hates sin and loves righteousness; that is the only attitude the Lord of love and mercy and wisdom and holiness could maintain toward sin and righteousness and remain just. Then, why do we pray? What is the purpose of prayer? It seems that we get closer to the truth when we say:

4. Prayer, real prayer, furnishes the Father an occasion to do for us just what his great, tender, throbbing heart longs to do. For the sake of clarifying and enforcing this thought, you will permit me to use a rather homely illustration from my own life. I was reared in a large, old-fashioned family. Doctor Broadus used to say that there are two ways of pronouncing family. One—family, consisting of man and wife; the other—family, is the scriptural way of pronouncing it. Ours was a family of twelve boys and four girls, two of whom died at an early age. You modern women will wonder how one little woman managed to mother fourteen to maturity. It was very simple, if you can see it. The children didn't spend their time in the picture shows. Each child had a definite duty to perform in home life, and mother and father did all of their "clubbing" at home. I re-

member to this day that hickory limb they kept over behind the kitchen stove, and have more painful memories of its frequent use. We had to work and all had to co-operate in our work to keep things going. I recall my special home assignment was in the kitchen. I had to help mother with such duties as dish-washing and churning. Those were dark and dreary days for me, but the memory of them lingers to bless and make brighter the passing days. Mother was like some sweet singing bird in the home. She had a song for every duty. I recall how I would tire out standing by the churn trying to pound butter out of stubborn milk. Then mother would come to my relief and start the song:

> How tedious and tasteless the hours
> When Jesus no longer I see!
> Sweet prospects, sweet birds, and sweet flow'rs,
> Have all lost their sweetness for me.

The most appropriate place on earth to sing that song is standing over a churn on a cold winter morning. Mother had so much to do that it was necessary to plan the work and to work the plan. She would cook the noonday meal and evening meal at the same time. Then she would carefully put away the evening meal in the old cupboard, and each child knew that trespassing in that department would be prosecuted. Yet the whole delegation would be hungry long before night. Mother would be sewing and singing, patching or spinning and singing, when we would all start up the chorus or cry for food. Mother would stand at the old spinning wheel and spin and sing. I shall never forget one of her favorite songs. It ran like this:

> Come, saint and sinner, hear me tell
> The wonders of Emmanuel,
> Who saved me from a burning hell
> And brought me here with him to dwell
> And gave me heavenly union.

Her very countenance carried evidence of that heavenly union, even as she was surrounded by hungry children, each crying, "Mother, I want something to eat." We didn't know any more about "reflex influence" than the modern mind seems to know about prayer, but we knew we were hungry and knew to whom to go when hungry. Nor did we inform Mother, or move her to change her attitude toward us. She knew more about our appetites than we knew ourselves, and certainly knew what would be good for each of us. There were Rufus, Robert, Elijah, Orlando, Noel, Daniel, Thomas, David, Felix, on down to James. They might have given us all Bible names, but they couldn't find enough easy names in the Bible. Mother knew exactly what each child would like and had our lunches already prepared. She knew what we would want and what we would need, even before we asked her. Our asking merely furnished her an occasion to do what she really wanted to do, and what she had previously planned to do for each of us.

Oh, if hungry hearts but knew it, our Father has already prepared just the blessing that each soul needs. He is waiting for us to assume the right attitude toward him. He wants to give us his best. But that suggests another question:

II. WHAT SORT OF PRAYING WILL FURNISH THE FATHER AN OCCASION TO GIVE US HIS BEST?

1. Isaiah (59: 1-4) tells us plainly that we cannot live ragged and godless lives and expect to get the ear and heart of the Father in time of need. "Behold, the Lord's hand is not shortened, that it cannot save; neither his ear heavy, that it cannot hear: but your iniquities have separated between you and your God, and your sins have hid his face from you, that he will not hear. For your hands are defiled with blood, and your fingers with iniquity; your lips have spoken lies, your tongue hath muttered perverseness. None calleth for justice, nor any pleadeth for truth; they trust in vanity, and speak lies; they conceive mischief, and bring forth iniquity." The Psalmist tells that if we even regard iniquity in our hearts, whether we commit the deed in actual experience or not, that we forfeit every right to claim and expect an answer to our prayers: "If I regard iniquity in my heart, the Lord will not hear me" (Psalm 66: 18). Jesus gave tremendous emphasis to the necessity of right living, when he said: "If ye abide in me, and my words abide in you, ye shall ask what ye will, and it shall be done unto you" (John 15: 7).

2. We must get right with men, too. Jesus makes it very plain that we cannot harbor hatred in our hearts for our fellow man and at the same time maintain the right attitude toward God. We must exercise forgiving grace if we would be forgiven. "And

when ye stand praying, forgive, if ye have aught against any: that your Father also which is in heaven may forgive you your trespasses" (Mark 11: 25).

3. We must really desire the things we ask for when we pray. "Therefore, I say unto you, what things soever ye desire, when ye pray, believe that ye receive them, and ye shall have them" (Mark 11: 24).

Nor is that all. The desire must be unselfish. James brings two grave indictments against Christians. He charges that we are spiritually impoverished, that life is empty and impotent and full of dull gnawing—not because God has failed to answer our prayers, but because we have refused to pray, or else we have failed to make our supplication in the right spirit. "Ye have not, because ye ask not. Ye ask, and receive not, because ye ask amiss, that ye may consume it upon your lusts" (James 4: 2, 3).

"The burning point of pain" for all Christendom today is not unanswered prayer, but un-offered prayer, or prayer offered with an improper motive. It is not an easy matter to purge our souls of selfishness even in praying for spiritual blessings. It may seem strange, but it is quite as difficult to pray for spiritual blessings unselfishly as it is to pray for temporal blessings unselfishly. We can readily see why the Father would wisely refuse to answer our prayers for temporal blessings to consume upon the lusts of the flesh. But, if more difficult to see, it is just as true that he will not hear our prayers and lavish spiritual blessings upon us unless we desire and are willing to use them for his glory. David gives us a splendid example in praying for spiritual blessings:

"Restore unto me the joy of thy salvation; and uphold me with thy free spirit. Then will I teach transgressors thy ways; and sinners shall be converted unto thee" (Psalm 51: 12, 13).

Ask God for anything that you are willing to use in his service and for his glory, and he will give you the thing asked for or something better.

4. Prayer must be offered "in the name of and for the sake of Christ." Indeed, it is not prayer at all unless we ask in reliance upon what he has done for us. It may be pleading for blessings through a selfish motive, but it is not prayer. We have no right to attach the name of Christ to a selfish petition. "And whatsoever ye shall ask in my name, that will I do, that the Father may be glorified in the Son" (John 14: 13).

5. And, finally, when we ask in his name, we should count the things as good as done. "If ye shall ask anything in my name, I will do it" (John 14: 14). When he says, "I will do it," it is as good as done. "Therefore, I say unto you, what things soever ye desire, when ye pray, believe that ye receive them, and ye shall have them" (Mark 11: 24).

There it is again—"Believe that ye receive them,"—count the blessings as good as received—appropriate them and rejoice in them, "and ye shall have them."

Have you observed how frequently David did the very thing we are here enjoined to do? We can hear him pleading his case with the Father—"O Lord, the hounds of hell are at my heels, they are digging pits for me. Oh, shield me, prevent blood-thirsty men from devouring me—uphold me with thy love—" and on and on. But you have doubtless noticed that in almost every instance, following such prayers, David breaks forth in a Psalm of praise in which he thanks God for doing the very things he has asked him to do. That is faith.

There comes to mind a beautiful scene and thrilling experience back in an early pastorate. It was a small town where the pastor could know every person in town by name. There was one good woman who stood out above us all as the most devout Christian in the community. She was the mother of a large family of fine sons and daughters. The entire family held membership in the Baptist church, except one wayward and reckless son.

Our annual revival meeting was in progress and this mother was greatly concerned about the condition of her one wilful boy. One day the pastor gave a rather strange invitation at the close of a morning service. There were a dozen unsaved people present, and the pastor urged upon those who could and would honestly indicate an interest in the matter of personal salvation to come to the front and linger for a special prayer. Several responded to that call, but the obstinate son of the noble mother was not among them. Those who witnessed the scene will never forget how wistfully she would look across to her son and entreat him with her very tears to come to Jesus. But he refused. Finally, the good old mother arose and made her way down to the altar to take her place with lost men and women. What did it all mean? Hear her explain it: "O pastor, I did want my boy at least to say that he wanted to be a Christian by coming to the front today. He refuses to come, so I came to represent my lost boy. The Father will see and understand and may it please him to save my boy today." We were all in tears, and soon upon our knees in prayer. Never in my ministry have I heard such an agonizing prayer for a lost soul as the old mother offered. But before she said "amen," she was praising God for the salvation of that boy. You are not surprised that the boy was at the altar confessing Christ before the prayer was finished. "What things soever ye desire, when ye pray, believe that ye receive them, and ye shall have them" (Mark 11: 24).

Chapter 6

THE LORD'S LOVE TEST

So when they had dined, Jesus saith to Simon Peter, Simon, son of Jonas, lovest thou me more than these? He saith unto him, Yea, Lord; thou knowest that I love thee. He saith unto him, Feed my lambs.

He saith to him again the second time, Simon, son of Jonas, lovest thou me? He saith unto him, Yea, Lord; thou knowest that I love thee. He saith unto him, Feed my sheep.

He saith unto him the third time, Simon, son of Jonas, lovest thou me? Peter was grieved because he said unto him the third time, Lovest thou me? And he said unto him, Lord, thou knowest all things; thou knowest that I love thee. Jesus saith unto him, Feed my sheep.—JOHN 21: 15-17.

OUR text is found in the climax of a simple incident that literally scintillates with striking suggestions and thrilling truths. We shall have to keep in mind the setting of the story if we would see its significance and do justice to the characters involved.

It is plain that Simon Peter has received far less than justice at the hands of preachers in the interpretation of the incident before us. The disciples were in Galilee to meet Jesus by a very special appointment made by Jesus in person prior to his crucifixion. They had been reminded of this appointment on two very special and spectacular occasions following his resurrection. They could not forget the plain and positive promise of Jesus to meet them in Galilee. They had trudged through the dusty thoroughfares from Jerusalem to Galilee in the radiant hope of expectancy. Had not Jesus promised to meet them in Galilee? Upon reaching the threshold of Galilee they swept the horizon, expecting the immediate appearance of their Lord, but Jesus was nowhere to be found. They searched through the quaint villages and verdant valleys and majestic mountains and were disappointed. Remembering his fondness for the restful calm of quiet lakes, they turned to the seaside. Again they were disappointed and perhaps a sense of despair settled upon them.

At this point they resolved to go fishing. Now those who have a disposition to play up Peter's perfidy have pounced upon this incident as positive proof that Peter's resolve to go fishing was tantamount to a renunciation of his allegiance to Christ. There is nothing in the text that justifies such an indictment against Peter. If we impugn the motive that prompted Peter's resolve to go fishing, we should at least remember that the other disciples voluntarily chimed in, "We also go with thee." And they did. They fished all night and "caught nothing," but when the morning was come they saw Jesus on the shore.

G. H. Morrison, of Glasgow, reminds us of how these words chime together—"night nothing," "morning master!" When we lose the conscious presence of Jesus, it is always night. One glimpse of Jesus will dispel dark clouds, and in his presence it is always light.

Thus Jesus found his tired, disappointed and depressed disciples in the early morning hour. He feasted them and then tested them. He turned Heaven's searchlight full upon their hearts and singled out Peter and put three personal, probing questions that struck home. These three questions provoke some other questions.

I. WHY DID JESUS CALL PETER BY HIS OLD NAME?

He was known as Simon as an unbeliever; as a Christian he was known as Peter. Had Jesus forgotten his impulsive disciple so soon? No, not that, but testing time had come.

1. Simon Peter had been signally honored, and had occupied prominent places in kingdom service, yet he needed the trial of testing. Most of us are prone to assume that the fact that we preach, teach, or serve in some conspicuous capacity settles the matter of our spiritual fitness. We appraise character by outward acts and forget that with God the merit or demerit of our acts is always determined by the motive that prompts them.

2. Simon Peter needed to be reminded of what he was by nature and of what sovereign grace had wrought within him. Peter was not only impulsive, he was proud and at times evidenced a disposition toward a haughty spirit. The spirit of haughty pride unfits a Christian for worth-while service. If there is anything destined to break the neck of our pride and hurl us into the dust of humility, it is just to be reminded that at best we are only sinners saved by grace. Doubtless Peter was all ears when he heard Jesus pro-

nounce his old name—"Simon, son of Jonas." His old name reminded him of his old life, his old loves, and his old allegiance. His new name reminded him of a new experience, a new fellowship, and new privileges.

3. Then Jesus called Peter by his old name to break the neck of pride and stir the note of gratitude in his heart. Common gratitude demands that we give to Jesus the unfeigned love and loyalty of our hearts. When Peter was reminded of how graciously God had bestowed boundless grace upon him, surely every note of gratitude in his heart responded in praise and service.

II. WHY DID JESUS MAKE LOVE THE BASIS OF HIS TEST?

1. Why did he not question the fact of Peter's denial? Had not Peter denied him with an oath? Why did he not ask, "Peter, will you promise not to deny me again? Will you promise not to use profanity again? Will you promise not to follow afar off?" Jesus never stops on the surface. He probes to the heart for the source of conduct.

2. Love is the supreme element of the Christian religion. It would not be saying too much to assert that Christianity is personified by and through a personal love for a personal Saviour. Other religions are based upon fear and force, or upon varied and sundry methods purported to lead to salvation by and through the observance of ritualistic rites. We do not become Christians by what we do, not even by what we do for God, but by what God through Christ does for us and in us. The one thing that characterizes a Christian is personal love for Christ.

That does not mean that every Christian, nor that any Christian, will love Christ as he ought. Christ's love test was destined to deepen Peter's love for Christ. He never appeals for deeper devotion, nor for sublimer service, on the basis of fear, but always on the basis of love. "If you love me, you will keep my commandments."

3. Christ was preparing Peter for a richer and fuller ministry among men. We often fail to exemplify the spirit of Christ in dealing with weak and imperfect Christians. When we see imperfections in the character of Christian comrades, we are too often prone to be harsh and critical. Christ was never harsh in dealing with weak Christians. "A bruised reed shall he not break, and smoking flax shall he not quench" (Matt. 12: 20). We should heed the admonition of Paul and thereby be more Christlike and most helpful to weaker Christians. "Brethren, if a man be overtaken in a fault, ye which are spiritual, restore such an one in the spirit of meekness; considering thyself, lest thou also be tempted" (Gal. 6: 1).

Dr. J. B. Tidwell, the great Bible teacher of Baylor University, related an incident to his class which illustrates what I am trying to say. A young father and mother had three children, two of whom were healthy and normal, but the third was mentally deficient. Each evening the children would wait and watch for the father to return from his daily work. One day as they waited and watched they saw him as he turned the corner, and the two normal children bounded away to meet him, leaving the deformed child toddling slowly and painfully in the distance. The father, with a tired body and aching heart, sat upon a rustic bench while the two fine children rushed about gathering wild flowers for him. The deformed child, with mind just enough to know that they were doing something for father, followed them, and by and by when two little chubby hands filled with choice flowers were extended with a hail, "Here, daddy! Here, daddy!" another little hand filled with grass and straw with a few crushed flowers was extended to daddy. The father reached over his normal children and pulled the weakling to his heart and cried, "God bless my poor unfortunate child." In the conduct of that father I seem to feel the heart-throb and see the attitude of Christ toward every weak and wayward Christian among us.

III. WHAT DID CHRIST MEAN BY "MORE THAN THESE"?

"Simon, son of Jonas, lovest thou me *more than these?*"

1. Those who interpret Peter's resolve to go fishing to mean that he had renounced his allegiance to Christ and his purpose to resume his old occupation tell us that Christ asked: "Peter, do you love me more than you love these fishing nets, tackle, and boat?" I am very sure that such an interpretation does violence to grace and gross injustice to Simon Peter. Granting that the grammatical construction permits such interpretation, there are two facts which forbid it.

(1). Christ would not make such a low and cheap comparison. It is preposterous to believe that he would compare the love a saved soul cherishes for the

Saviour with the love a Christian cherishes for a wet and bedraggled fishing net.

(2). The fact that Peter did not answer the question is positive proof that Jesus did not refer to either the fishing tackle or to fishing as a business. Peter knew exactly what Christ meant, and if he had meant fishing tackle, Peter would have given a positive answer without evading and ignoring the comparison. Peter's reply was not an answer to the Lord's question.

2. "More than these" evidently referred to the other disciples. Christ and the seven disciples were reclining in Oriental fashion around the breakfast spread upon the ground. Doubtless all eyes were focused upon Jesus. Jesus turned to Simon, with the other disciples in full view, and asked: "Simon, son of Jonas, do you love me more than these other disciples love me?" Now, we can see why Peter ignored the comparison and failed to answer the question. He was willing to declare his love for Christ, but was unwilling to declare the degree and depth of the love others cherished for him.

3. The idea that Christ meant to measure the love that Peter and the other disciples cherished for him on a comparative basis merely to upbraid and to humiliate Peter seems far-fetched and fanciful. True, Peter had declared on the night of the betrayal that, regardless of the conduct of others, he would not desert him. He did not declare his devotion to Christ was deeper than that of others, but that he was more resolute. To say that the test was staged to humiliate Peter would be a greater reproach to Christ than to a weak disciple. The test was not a trial to punish the dis-

ciples for any failure of the past, but a preparation for a more effective spiritual service in the future.

IV. WHY DID JESUS ASK THREE QUESTIONS?

We often hear it said that Jesus asked Peter the same question three times to counteract his threefold denial of Christ. In reality Jesus asked three separate and distinct questions.

1. The first question asked for a comparison. "Lovest thou me more than these?" Peter was prompt to reply, but did not answer the question.

(1). In his reply Peter did not use the same word for "love" as the word used by Jesus. He used a weaker word.

(2). As we have already observed, Peter ignored the comparison altogether. "Yea, Lord; thou knowest that I love thee."

While Peter did not answer the Lord's question in any true sense, he did make a commendable confession. His reply deserves more praise than censure. He had been too impulsive, too self-assertive, and too confident. He was not too confident of his love for Christ, but too sure of his ability to endure all—even death for Christ. Though he failed to make good in the crucial test, there is something commendable in his daring declaration. It at least revealed that he was willing to endure even severe ordeals for Christ. He overrated his fortitude, but didn't underrate his love and devotion for Christ.

2. In the second question, Christ dropped the comparison, but held to his strong word for love. Simon Peter would not say that he loved Christ more than

the other disciples loved him. Earlier in his Christian experience he might have blurted out an unreasoned affirmative answer. His failure now indicated that he was taming down and toning up. He could not use the Lord's strong word in declaring his love for him. He wanted to do so, but the word stuck in his throat. He reached for it, but the "reach exceeded his grasp." It is interesting to observe that in his later life he invariably used the Lord's strong word when expressing his devotion to Christ.

3. In the third question, Christ dropped his strong word for love and used Peter's weaker word, as much as to say: "Peter, I know all about the frailty of the flesh, I am not seeking to chide and shame you, but rather to correct and strengthen Christian character. Do you really love me as much as you claim to love me?" Then it was that Peter forgot all about restraint, and made a full-orbed, boundless confession. He acknowledged the prerogative of Christ as Lord of life to test the love of his own for himself and knew that neither vice nor virtue could escape his omniscient eye. Peter was painfully aware that his Lord knew all about the degree, the depth, and the quality of love his weak and sometimes wayward disciple cherished for him as Lord and Master. He did not know the full import or purpose of the testing, but he did know that his loving Lord had a beneficent purpose in it. That purpose was not to apprize the Lord of Peter's devotion to him, but was to perfect the quality and to deepen the degree of his devotion. As an aged Christian Peter looked back upon the trial of faith and the tests to which he had been subjected

and with an understanding heart he blessed God for the memory of them. "Wherein ye greatly rejoice, though now for a season, if need be, ye are in heaviness through manifold temptations: That the trial of your faith, being much more precious than of gold that perisheth, though it be tried with fire, might be found unto praise and honour and glory at the appearing of Jesus Christ: Whom having not seen, ye love; in whom, though now ye see him not, yet believing, ye rejoice with joy unspeakable and full of glory" (1 Peter 1: 6-8).

V. THE THREEFOLD COMMISSION

Although it is plain, as we have pointed out, that the Lord had perfect knowledge of Peter's love for him, yet it is equally clear that he wanted to hear him confess it. There is a distinction between a profession of love to Christ and confession of it. In profession the prominent person is the one who makes the profession; while in confession, "he whose name is confessed" is prominent.

Three times Jesus heard Simon Peter confess his love, and with each confession Jesus gives a definite commission.

1. "Feed my lambs." "You say you love me, and as you wisely concede I know the depth of your devotion for me; yet, I rejoice to hear you say it, and want to see you show it by carefully providing nourishment for my little ones." The tender emotions of Christ for young converts is implied in the terms of the Commission. His tenderness and patience in his dealing with Peter was meant as an object lesson

to be copied and an example to be followed by every undershepherd of souls.

2. "Shepherd my sheep." The terms employed in the threefold commission point out a purposeful and progressive idea in setting forward the importance of the varied functions and delicate duties of pastoral care. The "little ones" must not only be provided with seasonable, appropriate nourishment, but the more mature must be guided and directed in Christian service and protected from numerous foes that would prey upon them.

Christ, as the "good shepherd of souls," was Peter's ideal and example for every undershepherd or pastor. Peter's exhortation to all pastors is based upon the inspiration of this ideal. "The elders which are among you I exhort, who am also an elder, and a witness of the sufferings of Christ, and also a partaker of the glory that shall be revealed: feed the flock of God which is among you, taking the oversight thereof, not by constraint, but willingly; not for filthy lucre, but of a ready mind; neither as being lords over God's heritage, but being ensamples to the flock. And when the chief Shepherd shall appear, ye shall receive a crown of glory that fadeth not away" (I Peter 5: 2-4).

3. "Feed my sheep." Perhaps a better translation of this third commission would be: "Feed my little sheep." The thought seems to be of those in the flock who, though mature in years, have failed to develop in Christian character. They are weak and sickly. Like Peter, perhaps they have been subjected to temptations, and while faith did not fail, they faltered for lack of courage and have gone through life spiritually

marked and maimed by the mocking memories of miserable failures. Mature Christians who exemplify childlikeness in faith and spirit are a joy to a pastor's heart; but for a mature person to display a childish, babylike spirit constitutes a perplexing problem for any pastor. It is much more pleasant to provide spiritual nourishment for young, responsive Christians and direct the spiritual activities of the more developed and devoted Christians than it is to reprove and exhort the sickly of the flock. Peter says: "Even as Christ was patient, tender, and persistent in dealing with me as a weak and wayward disciple, so would I exhort all pastors. Be patient in duty whether duty be pleasant or painful, and when the chief Shepherd shall appear, ye shall receive a crown of glory that fadeth not away."

Chapter 7

GOD'S CLAIM, CHARGE, AND CHALLENGE

> Even from the days of your fathers ye are gone away from mine ordinances, and have not kept them. Return unto me, and I will return unto you, saith the Lord of hosts. But ye said, Wherein shall we return?
>
> Will a man rob God? Yet ye have robbed me. But ye say, Wherein have we robbed thee? In tithes and offerings.
>
> Ye are cursed with a curse: for ye have robbed me, even this whole nation.
>
> Bring ye all the tithes into the storehouse, that there may be meat in mine house, and prove me now herewith, saith the Lord of hosts, if I will not open you the windows of heaven, and pour you out a blessing, that there shall not be room enough to receive it.
>
> And I will rebuke the devourer for your sakes, and he shall not destroy the fruits of your ground; neither shall your vine cast her fruit before the time in the field, saith the Lord of hosts.—MALACHI 3: 7-11.

CERTAINLY the Christian ought to concede all that God claims on the basis of faith without so much as a question concerning the justice of the claim. The fact that God makes the claim ought to settle the matter. But every claim that God ever made for himself or for his own will stand up under the most painstaking investigation; every charge that he makes will stand the test of time and eternity; every challenge he issues has been verified a thousand times over.

Therefore, an honest investigation will make for our good and for his glory in substantiating these claims. What is his claim?

I. GOD CLAIMS THE EARTH AND THE FULNESS THEREOF

> The earth is the Lord's, and the fulness thereof; the world, and they that dwell therein.—PSALM 24: 1.

God has a threefold claim to the whole of earth and everything upon the earth.

1. He is the Creator of all. "In the beginning God created the heaven and the earth" (Gen. 1: 1). "For by him were all things created, that are in the heaven, and that are in earth, visible and invisible, whether they be thrones, or dominions, or principalities, or powers: all things were created by him, and for him: and he is before all things, and by him all things consist" (Col. 1: 16, 17). "Hath not one God created us?" (Mal. 2: 10).

2. He is the preserver of all. "By him all things consist" (Col. 1: 17). "O Lord, thou preservest man and beast" (Psalm 36: 6). "For in him we live, and move, and have our being" (Acts 17: 28).

3. He is the redeemer of all. "In whom we have redemption through his blood, even the forgiveness of sins" (Col. 1: 14). "What? know ye not that your body is the temple of the Holy Ghost which is in you, which ye have of God, and ye are not your own? For ye are bought with a price: therefore glorify God in your body, and in your spirit, which are God's" (1 Cor. 6: 19, 20).

Since we are his by right of creation, preservation, and redemption, who is man to gainsay his claim? He has a right to say: "For every beast of the forest is mine, and the cattle upon a thousand hills" (Psalm 50: 10). He has a right to say, "The silver is mine, and the gold is mine, saith the Lord of hosts" (Hag. 2: 8).

Then God is the owner of all that we use and enjoy here on earth. He has made man his steward. "Moreover it is required in stewards, that a man be found faithful" (1 Cor. 4: 2). God is good enough to man to permit him to get and use his wealth from the earth. But, mind you, man is a steward and it is required of him that he "be found faithful." "But thou shalt remember the Lord thy God: for it is he that giveth thee power to get wealth" (Deut. 8: 18).

It is here that much of our talk on "tithing" clashes with God's claim. We would not leave the impression that merely one-tenth of all that God gives us belongs to him. The whole ten-tenths belong to him, and we are merely his stewards. Then what of God's charge?

II. GOD CHARGES THAT HE WHO WITHHOLDS MORE THAN NINE-TENTHS OF THAT WHICH GOD GIVES HIM IS A ROBBER

> Will a man rob God? Yet ye have robbed me. But ye say, Wherein have we robbed thee? In tithes and offerings.—MALACHI 3: 8.

God says the whole earth is mine, the gold, the silver, cattle, lands, and so forth. But he permits man to use these material things which belong to him and gives man power to get wealth therefrom. But God expects one-tenth of the income from his own estate as an acknowledgment by man of God's complete ownership.

Let us suppose. Suppose God had made you, reader, a steward of one hundred acres of land. You enter into an agreement with a tenant to farm the land, you furnishing everything for one-half of all the land produces. At the end of the harvest you learn that the tenant has not delivered you one-half but only one-fourth of all the land produced. You would say that the tenant was a robber, and you would be justified in the charge. Well, God says: "It is my land, I furnish you the land and have also given you power to get wealth, and I require only one-tenth of all that I give you as an acknowledgment of my complete ownership." We never hear any Christian say that one-tenth is too much. If God can carry on his world-wide work—the biggest business on earth—with one-tenth of what he gives us, it does seem that we should be able to get by with nine-tenths. Some good Christians oppose tithing on other grounds; but none, so far as I have heard, on the ground that one-tenth is too much for a Christian to give. Indeed, many insist that inasmuch as the Jew was obligated to give one-tenth, the Christian ought to give more. But whatever may be said against tithing as a Bible standard of Christian giving, Abraham, Jacob, Moses, and Malachi all taught it and Jesus commended it. "Woe unto you, scribes and Pharisees, hypocrites! For ye pay tithe of mint and anise and cummin, and have omitted the weightier matters of the law, judgment, mercy, and faith: these ought ye to have done, and not to leave the other undone" (Matt. 23: 23). Jesus here says that judgment, mercy and faith are weightier matters than the matter of tithing. Certainly so! No thoughtful Christian will for a moment make the matter of tithing greater than faith. But doubtless Jesus would have said the same thing if the comparison had been between baptism and judgment, mercy and faith.

But the point to observe is that Jesus says you ought to have observed the matters of judgment, mercy, and faith, *and not to leave the other undone.* The "other" matter is the matter of tithing. "Ought" carries with it a sense of moral obligation. Then the teaching of Jesus is that the Christian is morally obligated not to neglect tithing.

Personally, I had rather undertake to prove, on a basis of Bible teaching, that every person, saint or sinner, is under obligation to tithe, because of the fact that he is a creature of God, and is preserved by his good providences, and is permitted to use that which belongs to God here upon earth, than to undertake to justify a Christian in failing or refusing to tithe.

No honest, serious-minded Christian contends that a tithe of his income is all that God requires of him. God says, "You are robbers if you withhold tithes and *offerings.*" The idea advanced here is that the Christian should bring his offerings as well as one-tenth of his income to the Lord's house.

It is clear that Bible teaching makes out a pretty bad case for all non-tithing Christians. But the case of the Christian who claims to tithe and who doesn't do it is even worse. The Bible says if you refuse to tithe you are a robber. But if you claim to tithe and do not, you are a robber and a liar, even to the Holy Ghost.

You recall the story of Brother Barnabas, who was an honored member of the First Church of Jerusalem. They had had a great revival meeting, the Spirit was upon the people, and church members became very liberal. That's nothing new—people are generally liberal under the influence of a spiritual revival. But Barnabas was the talk of the town. He sold everything he had and brought the money to the church. The revival broke out afresh. "And with great power gave the apostles witness of the resurrection of the Lord Jesus: and great grace was upon them all" (Acts 4: 33).

Mr. and Mrs. Ananias were members of that same church. They heard how Brother Barnabas was praised for his liberality and they coveted the praise, but didn't want to pay the price. So they talked it over and fell upon a plan of getting some of the praise without paying the price. They sold a possession and pretended to give the proceeds to the church, but they kept back part of the price. When Ananias got to the church, Peter met him at the door and said, "Ananias, why hath Satan filled thine heart to lie to the Holy Ghost, and to keep back part of the price of the land? . . . Thou hast not lied unto men, but unto God. And Ananias hearing these words fell down, and gave up the ghost: and great fear came on all them that heard these things" (Acts 5: 3-5).

About three hours later, Mrs. Ananias came in expecting some praise; but, instead of praising her, Peter preferred the same charge against her and she confessed and fell dead. They were both buried, "and great fear came upon all the church, and upon as many as heard these things" (Acts 5: 11).

Someone asks: "How did Peter know that they were frauds and cheats?" That's simple. If you claim to tithe and do not do it, you may put it down now that the people of your church know about it and you are regarded as a cheap pretender, a fraud, and a sham. You not only are not deceiving the Spirit, but you are not fooling the people about you.

But what of God's challenge?

III. GOD ISSUES A CLEAN, CLEAR-CUT CHALLENGE TO EVERY CHRISTIAN WHO WILL BE HONEST AND FAIR IN THE MATTER OF SUPPORTING HIS KINGDOM WORK

> Bring ye all the tithes into the storehouse, that there may be meat in mine house, and prove me now herewith, saith the Lord of hosts, if I will not open you the windows of heaven, and pour you out a blessing, that there shall not be room enough to receive it.
>
> And I will rebuke the devourer for your sakes, and he shall not destroy the fruits of your ground; neither shall your vine cast her fruit before the time in the field, saith the Lord of hosts.—MALACHI 3: 10, 11.

1. Note that the challenge is based upon the bringing of the tithes. What is a tithe? It is ten per cent of the net proceeds of all that God gives us, whether we are farmers, merchants, lawyers, doctors, teachers, or preachers,—ten cents out of each dollar.

2. Note that the tithe is to be brought into the Lord's house. "And all the tithe of the land, whether of the seed of the land, or of the fruit of the tree, is the Lord's: it is holy unto the Lord" (Lev. 27: 30). Now if the tithe is the Lord's, holy unto the Lord, then certainly he has a right to say when and where it shall be deposited. He has been just as explicit on this question as on the question of salvation by grace, or the question of baptism by immersion of a believer in water.

"They shall not appear before the Lord empty: every man shall give as he is able, according to the blessing of the Lord thy God which he hath given thee" (Deut. 16: 16, 17). That is in perfect accord with Paul's teaching in 1 Corinthians 16: 2, only Paul tells us exactly when we are to appear,—"Upon the first day of the week." That is, when they met for worship in Corinth, "let every one of you lay by him in store, as God hath prospered him."

Summing up, we see that the Christian is to give according as God has prospered him. But how much? What per cent? Unless we accept the standard of tithing as a minimum—with offerings in addition to the tithe, which was taught in the Old Testament and approved by Jesus in the New Testament—we do not know, and cannot know. Acting upon the best light we have, it is fair to say:

That the Christian is duty-bound to give a tithe; that he must bring it to the Lord's house—his place of worship. If it is the Lord's and you are his—a steward—you ought to be faithful and place that which belongs to him exactly where he says place it. If a

Christian accepts tithing as a scriptural basis of supporting kingdom work, then he has no moral right, and certainly no scriptural right, to scatter the tithe which is "holy unto the Lord" to dozens of other places and objects, no matter how desirable. "Bring ye all the tithe into the storehouse" ("mine house"). You can stand at your door or on the street and give away ten per cent of your income, or all of it, but that will not constitute scriptural giving.

3. We must give the tithe into the Lord's house on the first day of the week. We are not left to guess, but are told how much to give (a tithe), where we are to give it (mine house), and when (first day of the week). The honest Christian who accepts this challenge has the promise of his favor: "I will open you the windows of heaven." "I will pour you out a blessing." "I will rebuke the devourer for your sakes." "Your vine shall not cast her fruit before the time in the field." All of which is in line with the promise of Jesus: "Give, and it shall be given unto you; good measure, pressed down, and shaken together, and running over" (Luke 6: 38).

But, dear Christian friend, let us not commercialize these beautiful promises by thinking of them in connection with material things. There are so many blessings that money cannot produce or buy.

Let me take you into my confidence and tell you a little secret that has revolutionized my thinking concerning money and concerning giving. Somewhere I learned that every honest dollar I have ever earned is a part of my real self. I must put out in honest work my brain and nerves and muscle and energy to earn an honest dollar. Now, I can hold a dollar in my hand and say: "You are a part of my blood and brain and muscle and nerves. You are a part of myself. By energetic effort I have pulled you out of myself and molded you into this form for convenience." Then I take one dollar, or many dollars, to my altar of worship, and with a worshipful spirit say: "Lord, here is my offering today. It isn't much. I wish it were more, but it is a part of me–a part of the body and soul that thou gavest me. It is such a joy to put a part of myself upon your altar in such form as to be sent everywhere that Southern Baptists tell the story of thy love. I cannot go everywhere in person, but through this offering I am sending a part of myself to preach the gospel of thy redeeming grace here at home and out to the ends of the earth. Through this offering I rejoice to invest a part of my blood and brain and brawn in building church houses and schools; in feeding orphans, in caring for the old preachers who were underpaid and overworked, in training other lives to take their places in kingdom work, in healing the sick, in doing all that thou wouldst have me do, for I am thine–all thine. Amen."

Chapter 8

WHAT IS IN THE DARKNESS?

He revealeth the deep and secret things; he knoweth what is in the darkness, and the light dwelleth with him. —DANIEL 2: 22.

THE King of Babylon was grappling with a black and bitter midnight experience. He longed to know what was in the darkness. Like many of our day, he foolishly turned to the wrong source for help and his darkness deepened. Yet, he deserves more credit than the modern disciples of darkness who turn to mediums of spiritism. He at least refused to be a party to his own deception. He declined to divulge his dream, insisting that if the astrologers could tell its meaning they should be able to tell its subject matter. He imposed a condition that brought forth a commendable confession. "There is not a man upon the earth that can show the king's matter."

The darkness was dreadful and the king became desperate. In his rage he issued a cruel decree of death for all the wise men of Babylon. Daniel was the wisest man in Babylon, and the captain of the king's guard had his death warrant in his hand. Darkness! Dreary, dismal, desolate darkness settled like a pall over all Babylon. What is in the darkness? The king didn't know. The Chaldeans didn't know.

Daniel didn't know. But Daniel knew one who did know, and was wise enough to turn to him. He used his head in pleading with the king and then prayed to God to save his head from the hands of the king's executioner by revealing to him the king's dream and its meaning. His prayer was answered, and Daniel told the king the secret of his strange dream. And in his prayer of praise he points to one "who knoweth what is in the darkness."

I. HE KNOWS ALL ABOUT THE DARKNESS WITHIN

1. We are told that Socrates spent the best part of his life expostulating upon the one theme, "Know thyself,"—a happy theme for man's discourse, but a hopeless task to assign to any man. "Know thyself" was inscribed upon the Delphic Oracle as an imperative precept, but an impossible task. Pope, in his "Essay on Man," admonishes:

> Know thyself, presume not God to scan;
> The proper study of mankind is man.

But it all depends upon which man we study. Doctor Holmes, in *The Autocrat of the Breakfast-table*, wisely declares that whenever two men engage in conversation there are really six men present. There is the man as he really is, the real man. There is the man that each sees the other to be. Then there is the man that each sees himself to be. Only God knows the real man.

2. Therefore, if we would know what is in man, we must turn to him of whom it is said: "And (he) needed not that any should testify of man: for he knew what was in man."

There are secret depths in every human soul that have never been sounded by man. That is what we mean when we speak of our friends who have surpassed our fondest hopes, in evidencing a superior quality of courage and have been made "more than conquerors." It is a commonplace confession: "Well, the old boy made the grade. I didn't know he had it in him." We never know. Or, when the voice of anguish expresses bitter disappointment: "I thought I knew the man, but I never dreamed that he was capable of committing such a dastardly deed."

"I thought I knew." Why should I be so presumptuous? At best, man only looks upon the outward form. One can never look upon man and discover the designing, devilish schemes seething in a sin-diseased brain-box; nor solve the secret of suppressed emotions when the soul of man is in the grip of aching grief. "Know thyself." Impossible!

3. A wise admonition:

> Know thy Lord, presume not self to scan;
> Only God knows what there is in man.

David tells the whole story in Psalm 139: 1-4, 11, 12: "O Lord, thou hast searched me, and known me. Thou knowest my downsitting and mine uprising, thou understandeth my thought afar off. Thou compassest my path and my lying down, and art acquainted with all my ways. For there is not a word in my tongue, but, lo, O Lord, thou knowest it altogether. . . . If I say, Surely the darkness shall cover me; even the night shall be light about me. Yea, the darkness hideth not from thee; but the night shineth as the day: the darkness and the light are both alike to thee."

Thank God, somebody knows, and our hope is in him!

> Failing in strength when opprest by my foes,
> Somebody knows, Somebody knows;
> Waiting for someone to banish my woes,
> Somebody knows—'tis Jesus.
>
> Wounded and helpless and sick with distress,
> Somebody knows, Somebody knows;
> Longing for home and a mother's caress,
> Somebody knows—'tis Jesus.

II. HE KNOWS ALL ABOUT THE DARKNESS WITHOUT

1. Dark War Clouds.

War clouds are gathering again, and dropping their drapery of gloom over many nations of the earth. The grinding heel of godless greed is upon the defenseless heads of millions who hunger for bread. The curse of communism is seeking to spread a black wand of infidelity over all humanity.

We shudder as we read Maurice Hindus' gruesome story of godless Russia in *Humanity Thinking Red*, and Prokhanoff's *In the Cauldron of Russia*, or Kagawa's graphic delineation of the dreadful conditions in Japan. When we recall how Mussolini, the mad man of Italy, suffering from ego intoxication, looked with lustful eyes upon the gold in the hills of Ethiopia, then plunged his people into war and sacrificed peace upon the altar of greed in an act of national banditry, we are made to cry, "How long, O Lord!

How long?" When we see our own country floundering through what H. G. Wells calls the "days of frustration," seeking to drink herself into sobriety, and to borrow her way into prosperity, the darkness deepens. But for faith, such a dark picture would produce for me an incurable pessimism, and send me forth sobbing and sighing with the doleful poet:

> My life is cold and dark and dreary,
> It rains and the wind is never weary.
> My thoughts still cling to the mouldering past,
> And the hopes of youth fall thick in the blast.
> And my life is dark and dreary.

But an unwavering faith in the mercy, wisdom, and power of God saves me from despair.

One is reminded of the pessimism that fell as a pall upon Wordsworth following the French Revolution. He had hoped that the bloody battlefield would become the birthplace of something better. He had dreamed of the birth of brotherhood; of a nation shaking off her shackles, and in the full dignity of manhood declaring for freedom. And when those dreams were shattered, "I lost," says Wordsworth,

> All feeling of conviction, and in fine
> Yielded up moral questions in despair.

Men are beginning to learn that "there never was a good war nor a bad peace." Ninety-nine per cent of the bloody wars of the world have been mass murder in uniform.

God knows what is in the dense, dread darkness of war, and would teach us that war denotes devastation, degradation, and desolation for the nations of the world.

> If I were a Voice—a persuasive Voice—
> That could travel the wide world through,
> I would fly on the beams of the morning light
> And speak to men with gentle might,
> And tell them to be true.
> I'd fly, I'd fly o'er land and sea,
> Wherever a human heart might be,
> Telling a tale, or singing a song,
> In praise of the Right—in blame of the Wrong.
>
> . . . .
>
> If I were a Voice—a controlling Voice—
> I'd travel with the wind;
> And, whenever I saw the nations torn
> By warfare, jealousy, or scorn,
> Or hatred of their kind,
> I'd fly, I'd fly, on the thunder crash,
> And into their blinded bosoms flash;
> And, all their evil thoughts subdue,
> I'd teach them a Christian Brotherhood.*
>
> —*Charles MacKay.*

2. He knows about the darkness in your life and in mine. While preparing this message with the hope of comforting others, four letters came from friends in as many states, each telling the age-old story of soul anguish and heartache brought by sickness, sorrow, and dark disappointment. This, from a great and honored pastor: "The last sixty days have been the darkest days of my life. The doctor holds out no hope of recovery. We have talked it over in the

* From *Poems of Inspiration.* Copyright, 1925, Blue Ribbon Books, Inc. Used by permission.

home. It was hard, but God has been so gracious to us." My friend is saying in another language: "God has been with us all through these dark days." He has been, and he knows all about the darkness.

Another, concerning a great Christian mother: "We had to take mother back to the hospital. We do not know how it will turn out." No, my friend does not know what is in the darkness, but the Father knows all about it.

Here, another from a great Christian layman whose life has been a benediction to Southern Baptists: "It was a terrible crash. My car was completely demolished. Both lower limbs badly broken and several serious lacerations. I do not know how I got through alive, but I am rapidly recovering." It is the same old story—"I do not know." God does know.

And still another, concerning a very choice friend who does me the honor of calling me "her other pastor,"—a cultured, refined, and consecrated Christian whose very life has been a living sacrifice to sacred service: ". . . in the hospital again, perhaps for a lengthy stay . . . we do not know."

We never know, but, like Daniel, we know One who does know.

> So I go on not knowing;
> I would not if I might;
> I would rather walk in the dark with God
> Than to go alone in the light;
> I would rather walk with Him by faith
> Than to walk alone by sight.
>
> My heart shrinks back from trials
> Which the future may disclose,

Yet I never had a sorrow,
But what the dear Lord chose;
So I send the coming tears back
With the whispered word, "He knows."
—*Mary G. Brainard.*

3. He knows about the darkness of death. There is no gain in denial, there is darkness in death.

William Sidney Porter, better known as O. Henry, the brilliant but reckless son of the rugged hills of North Carolina, died in the afternoon of a bright June day. His last words were: "Turn on the light—I don't want to go home in the dark." Who would? Men live in, and love darkness rather than light, but no one craves to make that last lone journey in the dark. Ben Johnson expressed a great truth when he said: "Good men see death, the wicked taste it."

There is boundless comfort in that delicate suggestion of the familiar Psalm: "Yea, though I walk through the valley of the shadow of death, I will fear no evil: for thou art with me; thy rod and thy staff they comfort me."

"The shadow of death." The suggestion is that death comes just close enough to the child of God to cast a shadow across his pathway. Nor is that all—the fact of a shadow beneath suggests, yes, gives assurance of a light above. There can be no shadow below without a light above.

III. HE TURNS DARK CLOUDS INSIDE OUT

We are never disturbed about the darkness that gathers about those who oppose the will of God in life. We rather expect it. But what of the dark clouds of gloom that gather and hang like a dread pall over the lives of the friends of God?

1. There is the case of Joseph, God's perfect gentleman,—perhaps the only person in all sacred history without a blemish on his character, or in his conduct. Yet he lived under a cloud. It must have been dark for Joseph down in the well. But he was delivered. Yes, delivered into the hands of a devilish, designing woman. It is a good story of a dark beginning, but it has a glorious ending. Hear the climax of the matter: "Joseph is a fruitful bough, even a fruitful bough by a well; whose branches run over the wall: the archers have sorely grieved him, and shot at him, and hated him: but his bow abode in strength, and the arms of his hands were made strong by the hands of the mighty God of Jacob" (Gen. 49: 22-24).

"And Jospeh said unto them, Fear not: for am I in the place of God? But as for you, ye thought evil against me; but God meant it unto good, to bring to pass, as it is this day, to save much people alive" (Gen. 50: 19, 20).

2. Take the case of Moses, a model for meekness, God's chosen leader for ancient Israel. His life started in a raging storm of an ungodly king's wrath. It was dark when Moses was dealing with wicked old Pharaoh, but the darkness deepened when his own people turned against God. But God turned the dark clouds inside out and baptized a nation in light.

3. We started with the case of daring young Daniel, a man with a splendid spirit and spine. Doubtless others had made the discovery that "God knoweth what is in the darkness," but Daniel recorded the fact.

But why go on? Time would fail us to tell of patient Job, weeping Jeremiah, David, the man after God's own heart, the intrepid Paul, and gentle John. These all wrought valiantly for God in spite of darkness and lived to see the clouds rifted, then lifted and turned inside out.

What is in the darkness? There are literally millions of souls buffetted, beaten, and baffled by the perplexing problems of today and who plead for an answer to that age-old question, "What is in the darkness?" No one seems to know. But, after all, that is a matter of small moment. Knowing is not the main thing. Daniel didn't know, but he knew the *One* and the only *One* who "knowing what is in the darkness, and the light dwelleth with him." It is the privilege of one and all to know Daniel's God, "whom to know is life, and the life was the light of men." With unfaltering faith we follow the "Father of lights, with whom there is no variableness, neither shadow of turning" (James 1: 17).

> Lead, kindly Light, amid th' encircling gloom,
> Lead Thou me on!
> The night is dark, and I am far from home;
> Lead Thou me on!
> Keep Thou my feet;
> I do not ask to see
> The distant scene; one step enough for me.
>
> So long Thy pow'r hath blest me, sure it still
> Will lead me on
> O'er moor and fen, o'er crag and torrent, till
> The night is gone,
> And with the morn those angel faces smile,
> Which I have loved long since, and lost awhile!

Chapter 9

ALL FOR THE BEST

> There is therefore now no condemnation to them which are in Christ Jesus.—ROMANS 8: 1a.
>
> And we know that all things work together for good to them that love God, to them who are the called according to his purpose.—ROMANS 8: 28.
>
> Who is he that condemneth? It is Christ that died, yea rather, that is risen again, who is even at the right hand of God, who also maketh intercession for us.—ROMANS 8: 34.

HERE is one of the most difficult passages in the Bible for a Christian to understand, or even to believe, when the billows of adversity threaten to engulf and to overwhelm, or when the soul is in the "grip of aching grief." Yet it is possible that we would never see the spiritual significance of Paul's positive statement without viewing it from the valley of sorrow.

Paul begins his profound argument with the positive assertion, "There is therefore now no condemnation to them which are in Christ Jesus." That is a startling assertion. It was so startling to the translators of the King James Version that they were not willing to let it stand as Paul put it. It clashed with the teachings of the established church. They did not dare to change what Paul said; yet they did alter the clear implication of his statement by taking the last clause of verse four—"Who walk not after the flesh but after the Spirit"—and tying it on to verse one as a conditional, or modifying, clause. They were not satisfied with what Paul said and sought to modify it, thus making it harmonize with the theories of men. If the theories of men fail to harmonize with the Scriptures, that is no fault of Paul. It simply means that we need to abandon theories and adopt the Word of God. Paul is saying in substance what Christ says in John 5: 24: "He that heareth my word, and believeth on him that sent me, hath everlasting life, and shall not come into condemnation; but is passed from death unto life." Jesus simply states the sublime truth which must be accepted by faith. Paul affirms that Christ makes good his promise and then hastens to give proof based upon clear logic and personal experience. "There is now no condemnation to them which are in Christ Jesus. For the law of the Spirit of life in Christ Jesus hath made me free from the law of sin and death." When there is freedom from the law of sin and death, there can be no condemnation.

When separated from its context, there is something strange in the statement, "All things work together for good to them that love God"; but there is something sublimely satisfying in it for every believer who takes it as a logical deduction from Paul's argument and not as a detached declaration apart from his argument. We must observe exactly what he says and understand why he says it in order to appreciate its spiritual significance.

I. LET US OBSERVE EXACTLY WHAT PAUL SAYS

Doubtless most of our difficulties in studying the Scriptures grow out of the fact that we too often fail to observe exactly what the Holy Spirit actually says. Through superficial study we often imagine that a Bible text teaches certain things, or sometimes through a sinister spirit we try to make it mean certain things that are foreign to the text and false to the spirit of the Scriptures.

1. Paul says *all things* work together for good. Frequently we hear it said: "The Bible says everything works for good." No, it doesn't say *everything*, it says all things. Someone will say: "But all things include everything." Yes, but still Paul says *all things*, and has a reason for so doing. Why is it that we are tempted to associate this statement with only the darker experiences of life? When a Christian suffers some crushing blow, we are asked to harmonize the one ugly experience with Paul's declaration. Frankly, we cannot harmonize an isolated experience with Paul's *all things*, but we do know that God can take the one ugly experience along with all other experiences, good and bad, and make them work together for our good and for his own glory. There are certain cruel, tragic, and terrible experiences that would crush and kill any Christian if permitted to come into a life unguarded and unshielded by other preceding experiences. The point to observe is that God, in infinite mercy, wisdom, and power, shields, guards, and strengthens his own before the crushing, killing experience is permitted to come.

2. Paul says all things *work together* for good to them that love God. If I know what this scripture means, I also know when and where it was made plain to me. It was two o'clock in the morning, and a very dark night. I had stood by the bedside and watched my chum brother slip away to the other side. The fact that he was so young and buoyant in spirit made it doubly hard to see him die. The pathetic picture of a mother pleading for the life of her boy and frantically sobbing, "I cannot give him up," is yet vivid in memory. I can still hear the subdued tones of a father as he walked the floor half questioning the wisdom and mercy of God in his prayer, "O God, how I wish I could die for him! Why not take me and let him live?"

When a kindly neighbor announced, "He is gone," they pulled the sheet quietly and gently over his face. I felt that I must be alone. Facing my first crushing blow as a young Christian, I slipped away to the open spaces seeking light. I tried to pray, but it seemed more like mockery. I sobbed out, "O God," and then it was that Paul's statement literally leaped upon me. "All things work together for good to them that love God." It was sinful I know, yet I blurted out, "O God, how can it be for anybody's good, or for anybody's glory, for a young man with his high hopes, ambitions, and noble purposes and plans to be thus stricken down and swallowed up in death?" The sound of my own voice in the stillness of the night frightened me into silence and the "still small voice" seemed to whisper, "My child, the Lord does not say 'All things look good,' or that 'All things seem good,' or that 'All things feel good,' but that '*All things*, regardless of seeming appearance or feeling, the bright and the dark experiences, the sweet and the bitter, the good and the evil, work together for the good of them that love God.' "

Satan would take these dark, bitter, and ugly experiences and through them would strangle hope and destroy hope, if that were possible. We rejoice in the fact that Satan works only by the permissive will of God. Even Satan knows that his powers are limited in the life of the Lord's own. God does permit Satan to take possession of and use evil men in opposing spiritual forces. It was true in the case of Job, but Satan discovered that Job was shielded, "hedged about," by divine power, and God made the wrath of demon-possessed men to praise him.

3. Paul says all things work together *for good* to them that love God,—not because Satan would have it so, but because God in infinite wisdom and power will make it so. Satan pounces upon us, points out and emphasizes the bad experiences and only the bad experiences permitted to come into our lives. God emphasizes the fact that he takes "all things," the good and the bad, and makes them work together for the good of his own and for his own glory. He overrules evil with good. He brings sweet out of bitter, light out of darkness, and blessings out of bad experiences.

We are reminded of the story of a father whose only son was sick almost unto death. He had done all that he knew to do for the recovery of his child, who grew weaker with the passing of the dreary days.

Finally, he requested the family physician to call in a specialist for consultation. After the two physicians had carefully examined the patient, the specialist wrote out a prescription and asked the father to see to it that it was filled with only fresh medicines specified. The father would not trust another to go for the medicine. He went to his favorite pharmacists and called for the head prescription clerk and then asked permission to go behind the case and watch as the medicines were mixed. The clerk read the prescription with great care, and then spread it out before him and began to weigh and measure the various medicines called for. The anxious father stood by and prayed as each medicine was weighed out, "O God, grant that this medicine shall bring my boy back to health and strength." Again and again the prayer was repeated. Finally, the clerk took his mixer and pulled all the medicines into one pile on the plate and began to beat and stir it all together. Then the grief-stricken father looked on and said to himself: "Perhaps if any one of these various medicines should be taken alone into the system of my sick son, it might mean death." Then a new prayer was offered: "O God, grant that all these medicines taken together and working together shall bring my boy back to health." At best the father could only hope that the physician had rightly diagnosed the disease and that he had prescribed the right remedy.

Paul reminds us that the great Physician of souls knows all about the needs of his own, and in wisdom and love he will prescribe and administer the right remedy for every ill.

4. Paul is careful to say this applies only "to them that love God." It is rank fatalism to make it apply to all men. A true child of God can stand in the storm and sing with Ella Wheeler Wilcox:

> I know there are no errors
>   In the great Eternal plan,
> And all things work together
>   For the final good of man.
> And I know when my soul speeds onward,
>   In its grand Eternal quest,
> I shall say as I look back earthward,
>   Whatever is—is best.*

II. PAUL'S SOURCE AND STATE OF CERTAINTY

Why was Paul so positive? If he had said: "Maybe all things will take a turn for good," or "Let us hope for the best," we would not ask why? Paul is not guessing, nor does he deal in negations. He "nerves us with an eternal affirmative." His positive note gives assurance that he knows that all things work together for good to them who love God, and he also knows why it is so.

1. It must be so, because of the beneficent purposes of God for his own. "For whom he did foreknow, he also did predestinate to be conformed to the image of his Son." God has predetermined and named the final destiny of every believer. That destiny is perfect conformity to the image of Christ.

We do not look like Christ now, and sometimes we do not even act like Christians, but it is the open and

* From *Poems of Pleasure*. Used by permission, W. B. Conkey Co., Hammond, Indiana.

avowed purpose of God to purge his own of every trace of sin and finally bring them into the perfect likeness of Christ. It may, and does often seem that God's purposes have been frustrated, but it is never really so. When he predestinates a thing, it is as good as done.

2. Paul points out that this is a part of God's plan in executing his purpose for those who love him. It was not an afterthought, but was a part of his plan even from the foundation of the world. His plan was foreordained as well as the calling, the justification, and the ultimate glorification of every believer in Christ.

Dr. B. H. Carroll covers the case when he says: "Before there was any world, a covenant of grace was entered into between Father, Son, and Holy Spirit, the evidences of which covenant are abundant in the New Testament, and the parts to be performed by each person of the God-head are clearly expressed, namely: The Father's grace and love in agreeing to send the Son, his covenant obligation to give the Son a seed, his foreknowledge of this seed, his predestination concerning this seed, his justification and adoption of them here in time. Then the Son's covenant was the obligation to assume human nature in his incarnation, voluntarily renouncing the glory that he had with the Father before the world was, and in this incarnation of humility to become obedient unto the death of the Cross.

"The consideration held out before him, as a hope set before him, inducing him to endure the shame of the Cross, and the reward bestowed upon him because of that obedience, was his resurrection, his glorification, his exaltation to the royal priestly throne and his investment with the rights of judgment, and then the Spirit's covenant obligations were to apply this work of redemption in calling, convicting, regenerating, sanctifying, and raising from the dead the seed promised to the Son, the whole of it showing that the plan of salvation was not an afterthought; that the roots of it in election and predestination are both in eternity before the world was, and the fruits of it are in eternity after the judgment."

3. Paul points to the fact that God is for us as final proof of his contention. His argument is that since God is for us, it matters but little who may be against us. And that God is for us is evidenced by the fact that "he spared not his own Son, but delivered him up for us all, how shall he not with him also freely give us all things?" Since God so loved us that he gave his only begotten Son that whosoever believeth on him should not perish, but have everlasting life (John 3: 16), and since Christ gave himself for us that he might redeem us from all iniquity (Titus 2: 13, 14), therefore every believer is privileged to sing with David. "The Lord is on my side; I will not fear: what can man do unto me?" (Psalm 118: 6.)

> The soul that on Jesus hath leaned for repose,
> I will not, I will not desert to its foes;
> That soul, tho' all hell should endeavor to shake,
> I'll never, no, never, no, never forsake!

III. PAUL'S COMPREHENSIVE CHALLENGE

1. He challenges all the forces on earth, in heaven above, or in hell beneath, to bring a charge of condemnation against God's elect, that will stand up in the final judgment. When God justifies a believing sinner, it means that in Christ that sinner is acquitted. The verdict is rendered by the Supreme Judge and is irreversible. It is recorded in the Book of Life, which is "a register of judicial decisions already rendered."

2. In his defense of the believer's eternal security, he piles proof upon proof and stands upon the pinnacle of his pyramid of love and logic and defies all the forces of hell to storm the soul's fourfold fortress of faith. The soul's security is based upon: (1) The fact that Christ died for us; (2) the fact that he conquered death and came out of the grave; (3) the fact that he ascended to the right hand of God as our advocate; (4) and "who also maketh intercession for us" (Romans 8: 34).

C. H. Spurgeon speaks of this passage as the four pillars upon which rests the whole superstructure of salvation. Any one pillar is of sufficient strength to bear the weight of the world's sin. When Satan accuses and assaults, we have but to point to the Cross of Christ. The fact that Christ took our place under the law and was made to be sin for us and died in our stead should forever silence the accuser. If that does not suffice, surely the empty grave will strike him dumb. Paul stood by the Cross and dared Satan, then stood by the open, empty grave and shouted defiance in the face of death. "O death, where is thy sting? O grave, where is thy victory? . . . Thanks be to God, which giveth us the victory through our Lord Jesus Christ."

He died for us, but "Yea, rather he is risen." We are trusting and depending upon a risen, living, reigning Lord. "For, if, when we were enemies, we were reconciled to God by the death of his Son, much more being reconciled, we shall be saved by his life" (Romans 5: 10).

Nor is that all, the crucified and risen Lord is "even at the right hand of God, who also maketh intercession for us." With the Holy Spirit for us (verse 26), with God the Father for us (verse 3), and with Christ for us (verse 34), of whom shall we be afraid?

3. Christ not only conquers the evil forces that fight against us, but he overrules and uses them in making us more than conquerors. Paul names the common forces and factors which Satan has used through the ages to frustrate the purposes of God: tribulation, distress, persecution, famine, nakedness, peril, and the sword. He had experienced most of them. Yet he declares these things not only fail to conquer Christians, but are used of God in the strengthening of Christian fortitude and for the furtherance of Christianity. After issuing his challenge to the more common foes, he takes a still wider sweep and includes the foes of every realm: "Neither death, nor life, nor angels, nor principalities, nor powers, nor things present, nor things to come, nor height, nor depth, nor any other creature, shall be able to separate us from the love of God, which is in Christ Jesus our Lord."

Paul is in perfect harmony with the promises of

Christ to his own. "And I give unto them eternal life; and they shall never perish, neither shall any man pluck them out of my hand. My Father, which gave them me, is greater than all; and no man is able to pluck them out of my Father's hand" (John 10: 28, 29).

A mighty fortress is our God,
  A bulwark never failing;
Our helper He, amid the flood
  Of mortal ills prevailing.
And tho' this world, with devils filled,
  Should threaten to undo us,
We will not fear, for God hath willed
  His truth to triumph through us.
    —*Martin Luther.*

Chapter 10

THE SAINT'S DISTRESS SIGNAL

And his disciples came to him, and awoke him, saying, Lord, save us: we perish.—MATTHEW 8: 25.

And he was in the hinder part of the ship, asleep on a pillow: and they awake him, and say unto him, Master, carest thou not that we perish?—MARK 4: 38.

And they came to him, and awoke him, saying, Master, master, we perish. Then he arose, and rebuked the wind and the raging of the water: and they ceased, and there was a calm.—LUKE 8: 24.

OUR texts tell the tragic story of a terrible storm at sea. It was not unusual for storms to break upon this particular sea, but this one was unusually severe. The word used to designate it literally means an earthquake, as if the foundations were suddenly broken up. The disciples and the Lord were in a small, frail boat when the storm struck. The Master had requested the disciples to launch out and cross over to the other side. He must have been tired and sleepy following a strenuous season of teaching. He was fast asleep in the stern of the ship when the sea was so beaten into a furor that the roaring, raging waves resembled the teeth of mad dragons.

We are not surprised that the disciples were frightened. There is no danger that will make a person feel so helpless and inadequate as when he is caught in a storm at sea in a frail vessel. The disciples were frantic with fear when they rushed upon the Master. In their appeal for help each evidenced his individual reaction to danger. There are four lessons that loom large on the surface of the story.

I. THE THREE DISTINCT DISTRESS SIGNALS

1. There is no discrepancy or disagreement in the records of the incident. Those whose primary interest in the Bible is that of finding discrepancies invariably miss the deeper meaning of its message. They tell us that Matthew, Mark, and Luke clash in their respective reports of this incident. Then, instead of seeking a rational explanation of a seeming clash, they jump to the conclusion that the Bible is not inspired, and therefore not trustworthy.

It is easy to see that there is a difference in the three reports, but there is no clash, as we shall see later. The seeming discrepancies in the Bible that rationalists have made so much of are in reality plain indications, if not proof, that the Scriptures were written by men divinely inspired. That is exactly what the Bible claims for itself and what its friends claim for it. The difference in the reports of the Gospel narratives merely proves the independence of the inspired writers. It is positive proof that there was no collusion on the part of these writers. It also makes the record more replete, more trustworthy, and more glorious.

Suppose that Matthew, Mark, and Luke, in recording the incidents common to the Synoptic Gospels, had written from one and the same viewpoint and had used the same language in their respective records. Then what? We would have but one Gospel record instead of three; the others would have been mere repetitions.

2. There is no seeming clash in the incident before us. We have three separate reports of an historic fact. When the disciples rushed upon Jesus pleading for help, they were all talking. One was saying one thing; another, another. What actually happened was, each inspired writer recorded the thing that impressed him most. Matthew was impressed with the plaintive plea: "Lord, save us; we perish." Luke was more impressed with the cry: "Master, master, we perish." Mark was moved by the querulous question: "Master, carest thou not that we perish?"

3. The reaction of individuals in crises reflects and reveals character qualities. The fact of varied reactions on the part of individuals is well known to psychologists, but the exact reason for the wide variation is still an open question. Doctor Guenther of Berlin is now making a special study of the psychological factors involved in terror. The investigation is sponsored by the German government looking toward a scientific method of controlling groups so as to prevent panics.

If each of the inspired writers had given the name of the disciple who impressed him most with his plea for help, we would at least have a clearer knowledge of the character of each disciple. For instance, Matthew reports the reaction of an individual or a group facing perils and yet not forgetting the way out, "Lord, save us; we perish." Luke reports the reaction of those who become frantic when facing perils and who lose sight of everything else except perishing, "Master, master, we perish." While Mark tells of the character altogether too common in every age—those who would accuse God, and pass judgment upon his love and power to make good his claims for himself,—"Master, carest thou not that we perish?"

II. THIS INCIDENT REVEALS THAT CHRIST IS HUMAN AS WELL AS DIVINE, AND DIVINE AS WELL AS HUMAN

1. The Master is tired and falls asleep. There is humanity. He awakes and calmly commands the storm. "Peace, be still," and the winds and waves obey him. There is deity. Deity and humanity are perfectly blended in one sublime personality. Sleeping on the cushion in the stern of an old boat, he presents a picture of a tired, overworked man; commanding a storm and quelling mad waves, he presents the picture of the inexhaustible infinite One.

2. This is characteristic of the Gospel records. Wherever we find an incident emphasizing his humanity, we will invariably find evidence of the fact of his deity close by. This truth is confirmed from his humble birth in Bethlehem to his glorious ascension.

See him as a helpless babe in his mother's arms and hear the world exclaim: "Is this not the child of Joseph and Mary?" But wait! Hear the shepherds tell how the angel came and announced his birth: "And the angel said unto them, Fear not: for, behold, I bring you good tidings of great joy, which shall be to all people. For unto you is born this day in the city of David a Saviour, which is Christ the Lord. And this shall be a sign unto you; Ye shall find the babe wrapped in swaddling clothes, lying in a manger" (Luke 2: 10-12). Hear the wise men tell the story of how they were strangely guided by a star to the city of Bethlehem, and we are made to exclaim: "What manner of babe is this?" See him as a lad at the carpenter's bench—and we think of thousands of others in similar circumstances; but follow him to the Temple when he is twelve years of age and hear him asking and answering questions that baffled the most learned of his day, and we are convinced that he was supernatural. Stand on the banks of the Jordan and see John bury Jesus beneath the baptismal waters along with multitudes of others, and hear the world say: "Just a pious peasant obeying a religious rite." But wait! See the Spirit in the form of a dove descending upon him and hear the majestic voice from heaven approving the deed and claiming Jesus as his very own: "Thou art my beloved Son, in whom I am well pleased"(Mark 1: 11). Go with him to the grave of his friend Lazarus and see the tears of sympathy trickle down his cheeks. Surely he is human! But wait! Hear him cry: "Lazarus, come forth," and the pallor of the grave leaves his face as the flush of health leaps to his cheek. The luster of light and life flash from eyes that were languid in death. Lazarus, though dead, heard his Master's majestic voice and quit the tomb.

Again, follow him to the Cross and hear the mongrel group mock him, see them mutilate and mar his sinless body. See him hang like a helpless victim upon a Roman cross. They chide and jeer him: "If thou be the Son of God, come down from the cross." The challenge passed and now he is dead. There is no denying the fact he is dead. The death certificate was signed by competent authority, and like any other man his body is consigned to the tomb. He was human, but died the death of a common criminal. But, thank God, the story of Jesus does not end at a grave! Three days, dreadful, dreary and dismal days, drag by and an angel appeared and rolled back the stone from the door of the grave and sat upon it, thus showing his contempt for death. He did not roll the stone away from the grave so that Jesus could get out, but that friend and foe might look within and see that he was already out. He was committed to the grave as a victim, but he conquered death and came out of the grave as a victor.

"What manner of man is this, that even the winds and the sea" and disease and demons and death obey his voice. He was man plus. He was the universal man, and God of the universe. He was and is the God-man. Looking from heaven, he is God's way down to man, and looking up to heaven he is man's way back to God. As believers, we can shout with Richard Watson Gilder:

> If Jesus Christ is a man,–
> And only a man,–I say
> That of all mankind I cleave to Him,
> And to Him I will cleave alway.
>
> If Jesus Christ is a god,–
> And the only God,–I swear

I will follow Him through heaven and hell,
The earth, the sea, and the air! *

III. THIS STORY SERVES TO SHOW US THAT THE PATHWAY OF DUTY MAY BE PLAIN YET DIFFICULT

1. It is often false and sometimes fatal for a Christian to assume that he must be running counter to God's will in life, because there are difficulties looming up in the way. A young man confesses with an air of perfect complacency: "I offered myself for special service and entered school for special training, but it seemed that everything was against me, so I concluded that God didn't want me for special service. I have given up the idea." Such false reasoning would have led the last disciple to turn back. If Satan could have succeeded in implanting such false notions in the hearts of all believers, there never would have been a martyr to the cause of Christianity. It is well enough that the dilettante, seeking a place of selfish ease, turns back from the ministry. Christ has never promised to his servants a primrose path of ease and plenty. He has promised strength to overcome hardships, and grace to sustain us here and a crown of glory hereafter.

The bloody Bishop Bonner of London described the gruesomeness and pain connected with burning at the stake in an effort to persuade brave John Audly to recant, and the cowardly bishop could never understand the quality of courage that prompted John Audly to shout: "If I had as many lives as there are

* From "The Song of a Heathen." Used by permission, Houghton Mifflin Co., Boston.

hairs on my head, I would lose them all in the fire before I would lose Christ."

2. Difficulties in the way of Christian service do not necessarily mean that we have displeased God. "What have I done to bring this calamity upon me just when the prospects for Christian service seemed brightest and best?" The storm shrieks its answer and the disciples declare with a voice of assurance born of experience, "Nothing at all." But it is possible that you magnify and aggravate your lot by missing the meaning of the storms that break upon you.

3. It is possible, and even probable, that the way of Christian service is beset with difficulties because we are pleasing God.

Dr. G. Campbell Morgan calls our attention to the fact that the words Jesus used in rebuking the wind and commending the waves suggest that there was something demoniacal in that particular storm. It is at least worthy of note that Jesus used the same word in rebuking the wind that he used in rebuking the demon that cried out against him in Capernaum. "Let us alone; what have we to do with thee, thou Jesus of Nazareth? art thou come to destroy us? I know thee who thou art, the Holy One of God." And Jesus rebuked him. Now the fact that he employed the same word in rebuking the storm is at least suggestive. We know that a Christian displeases Satan when he pleases God, and we should know that demons use anything and everything at their command in an effort to frustrate the will and the plans of God in our lives. If we serve God acceptably, we must do so in spite of and over the protest of demons.

The storms that broke upon Job were sent by evil forces, and because of the fact that he feared God and eschewed evil. Job was in trouble, not because he displeased God, but rather because he had resolved to serve him regardless of the cost. If storms beat upon us because we are in his service, we may be sure that he will sustain us with his grace and in due time he will rebuke the storm.

> O Jesus, once rocked on the breast of the billow,
> Aroused by the shriek of despair from the pillow;
> Now seated in glory, the poor sinner cherish
> Who cries in his anguish, Save, Lord, or we perish.
>
> And O, when the whirlwind of passion is raging,
> When sin in our hearts his wild warfare is waging,
> Then send down thy grace thy redeemed to cherish,
> Rebuke the destroyer. Save, Lord, or we perish.

IV. STORMS AND DIFFICULTIES DO NOT ARGUE THAT JESUS HAS DESERTED US

1. We are never disturbed about the storms that break upon those who deliberately run counter to God's will. We recognize that the disobedient deserve to be dealt with drastically. Jonah knew God's will, but set his heart against doing his will. God commissioned him to go to Nineveh, but Jonah defied God and rose up to flee unto Tarshish. It seems that he expected to run into difficulties in seeking to run away from God. He at least recognized the storm as a judgment against him. Storms may argue that we have deserted God, but they never argue that God has deserted us.

2. It is not so easy to understand the storms that

beat upon the innocent and obedient. The disciples were not running away from God, but were going with him. The Master had expressed a wish to "pass over unto the other side," and his wish commanded them. Here we enter the realm where Christians are constantly assailed by perplexing problems and questions. Why does God permit evil forces to harass and hamper his own, and often his noblest servants? We cannot question his power over evil forces. We would not question his love and wisdom; but our very faith provokes the question, Why?

One of our truest and most faithful missionaries in Brazil went out as a Christian layman. He had not thought of preaching, but he loved the Lord and the lost and went out to re-enforce the gospel ministry as a Christian teacher. His very life preached wherever he went. It was not long before he was pressed into service as a preacher. His testimony was effective from his first message. Souls were saved. He was convinced that the natives needed to know the message of life more than they needed to know modern methods of living. He heard and answered the call to preach and went back into the interior and began a gloriously fruitful ministry. But alas, just in the crucial hour of his ministry he and his entire family were stricken down by a terrible yellow fever plague. Death claimed one of his children and played havoc with the little band of believers. We wonder if he was tempted to turn back? We know that he did not turn back, and thousands of native Christians are praising God that he held on and pressed on, but doubtless he was perplexed by many cruel questions that surged in his soul.

Paul had a similar experience. He had the inner urge to go to Rome, purely for the sake of releasing springs of influence that he knew would vibrate to the ends of the civilized world and for the glory of Christ. He had been encouraged by visions fresh from Heaven to make the journey, but was entreated not to do so, even by prophecies of coming evil. The urge was upon him—"I must see Rome." He set out for the imperial city via Jerusalem, the most direct route. He reached Jerusalem and was imprisoned in the castle of Antonia. The Lord appeared to him the second night of his imprisonment and gave him new assurance that he would yet see Rome. Yet he had to go through two years of imprisonment, suffer shipwreck at sea and endure a long delay in Malta before he reached Rome. All the while he was in the path of duty. Duty was very plain, but very difficult.

3. It is plain that God permits the winds of adversity to beat upon us and that sometimes he sends us into the teeth of the storm, but that is far from saying that he permits evil forces to frustrate finally his plans and purposes concerning his own. The question is raised, since Jesus is God, he knew that the storm would break upon them, then why did he send them into it? He sent them because he did know. He knew all about the storm. He knew what the end would be. He knew that they would be in dire distress, and yet never in danger. The truth is admirably expressed by William Cowper:

RADIANT REALITIES

God moves in a mysterious way
  His wonders to perform;
He plants His footsteps in the sea,
  And rides upon the storm.

Deep in unfathomable mines
  Of never-failing skill.
He treasures up His bright designs,
  And works His sovereign will.

Ye fearful saints, fresh courage take,
  The clouds ye so much dread
Are big with mercy, and shall break
  In blessings on your head.

Judge not the Lord by feeble sense,
  But trust Him for His grace;
Behind a frowning providence
  He hides a smiling face.

His purposes will ripen fast,
  Unfolding every hour;
The bud may have a bitter taste,
  But sweet will be the flower.